Words the Turtle Taught Me

Susan Richardson

with illustrations by Pat Gregory

CinnamonPress

INDEPENDENT   INNOVATIVE   INTERNATIONAL

Published by Cinnamon Press, Meirion House, Glan yr afon, Tanygrisiau, Blaenau Ffestiniog, Gwynedd, LL41 3SU. *www.cinnamonpress.com*

ISBN: 978-1-909077-71-3

British Library Cataloguing in Publication Data. A CIP record for this book can be obtained from the British Library.

Front cover design by Pat Gregory. Designed and typeset in Palatino by Cinnamon Press. Printed in Poland.

Cinnamon Press is represented in the UK by Inpress Ltd *www.inpressbooks.co.uk* and in Wales by the Welsh Books Council *www.cllc.org.uk*

Acknowledgements

Thanks to the editors of the following anthologies and journals in which some of the poems in this collection first appeared: *Nature & Myth* (Corbel Stone Press); *Nature & Language* (Corbel Stone Press); *Nature & Sentience* (Corbel Stone Press); *Driftfish* (Zoomorphic); *The Hopper* (Green Writers Press); *Some Cannot Be Caught* — *The Emma Press Book of Beasts*; *Dark Mountain, Issue 10* — *Uncivilised Poetics*; *Wild Atlantic Words* (Hungry Hill Writing); *The Emma Press Anthology of the Sea*; *Animal* — *a Beast of a Literary Magazine*; *Plumwood Mountain* — *An Australian Journal of Ecopoetry and Ecopoetics*; *The Learned Pig*; *Marine Conservation*; *SurVision Magazine*; *The Lampeter Review*; *Zoomorphic*; *Dark Matter—Women Witnessing*.

'Afterworld' was commissioned by World Animal Day, and text and audio versions of this poem, 'Waste' and 'De-extinct' feature on the World Animal Day website (*www.worldanimalday.org.uk*). 'Scar' was included in the *Do You Speak Seagull?* exhibition at the ONCA Centre for Arts and Ecology in Brighton.

Huge thanks, too, to the Marine Conservation Society for the opportunity to be their Thirty Threatened Species project poet-in-residence, and special gratitude to Debbie Stenner, marketing manager during the early months of my residency, for her enthusiasm and vision.

About the Author

Susan Richardson is a poet, performer, educator and editor, whose three previous collections, *Creatures of the Intertidal Zone*, *Where the Air is Rarefied* and *skindancing*, are also published by Cinnamon Press. In addition to her recent residency with the Marine Conservation Society, she is currently poet-in-residence with both the global animal welfare initiative, World Animal Day, and the British Animal Studies Network. Susan has performed at festivals throughout the UK, for organisations such as WWF and Friends of the Earth, on BBC 2, Radio 4 and at universities both nationally and internationally. She co-edits *Zoomorphic*, the digital literary magazine that publishes work in celebration and defence of wild animals. *www.susanrichardsonwriter.co.uk*

About the Artist

Pat Gregory is a printmaker, illustrator, crafter and gardener who has exhibited in Wales and England for over twenty-five years. She's a member of the Roundhouse Partnership, a group which has bought some acres of land near Cardiff to develop an orchard and forest garden and to learn woodland management skills. Her cards and other artwork are on sale both on occasional Roundhouse stalls and via her website: *www.patgregoryart.co.uk*

Contents

Least Concern

Fluke

Tursiops truncatus

For the first half-hour, we synchronise our binos
and our grey mistakes when spying
rocks and wrack.

One hour in, we vow to veto tuna.
Our guide tries to toss doubts aside and strand
them on a spit,
yet spirits sag like jellyfish.

We hold our breath for six minutes,
start to navigate the deck by clicks.
A woman who's fixed
what we insist is joy on her lips
offers up the crystals
which cling to her neck and wrists.

Mid-trip. Still no sign. So our guide's obliged
to summon Poseidon
but he comes without his ride,
while a guy who's dived in Cairns and Thailand yawns,
shuts down half his brain,
and wakes to name his thumb after a thermos.

Then, just as our pod of time leaps by,
my eyes, I find, can breach the t-shirts, shorts,
the flops and flips, can see the part-
digested chips, the seeds of refund pleas,
the woman's pique at her lack of healing.

A child, her stomach stuffed with bubble rings,
begins to cry.

Scar
Phoca vitulina

Cliff at full stretch.
Gorse grazing face.
Twitch of a frayed grayling.

Watching a seal beach herself beyond
          the sea's reach,
her skin's narrative punctuated
with scrapes and nicks — comma, colon,
quote mark, asterisk —
plus one hyperextended hyphen,
emphatic underline, overlong minus sign.

Shift stiff legs.
Jag of rock nags left hip
like an unanswered question.

It's a scar the shape of a fish farmer's blame
for his filched salmon stocks,
deep as his commitment to fire a fatal shot,
as our fixation with propellers and plastic.
It's one axis of a graph that exhibits her decline.
A horizon from which the sun
          can't bring itself to rise.
It's the line that must never be crossed.

Volunteer
Phocoena phocoena

start time eight a.m.
visibility one mile
sea state three to four

Snorts of wind try to tug his recording sheet from the security of
its clipboard. He'd like to weigh it down, anchor it with his first
definitive glimpse of the UK's smallest cetacean. But so far on this
clifftop watch, nine fishing boats aside, he's spied just a shape that
may or may not have been a wave, shadows of the rounded bodies
of clouds, the blunt rostrum of a buoy.

eleven fifteen
wind direction west-southwest
swell height moderate

There's nowhere on this form for him to record the boredom.
Nowhere to report the could-have-beens, the yawns, unsures, the
it-happened-too-quick-to-see. Nowhere to sort his IDs into a marine
species hierarchy — the one he's supposed to find today ranking,
in his mind, higher than seal, but lower, by far, than dolphin. And
nowhere to log guilt's scalene fin as he spots a *seagull!* wheeling over
the sea, instead of *kittiwake! lesser black-backed! herring!*

something past midday
self state stiff to fidgety
sandwich count's reached three

As he switches from cross-legged to kneeling, a blackthorn twig
breaches the surface of his track pants, spiking his right shin and
knee. His fingers, temporarily free of binoculars and pen, seek
spring squill's softness instead, with its doodles of blue flowers and
scribbled stems.

He sighs. Brushes crumbs from the recording form. Rummages in
rucksack for crisps and Gatorade. Sip — swallow — sip — swallow
— while his eyes, as if trapped as the incidental catch of a gillnet, are
dragged back to the sea and

no flashy leap
from the water
no re-entry splash

but broad hint
of fin   inkling
of back and

calf   half
an after-
thought

mirroring
its mother's
movements.

His preference for spotting dolphins draws in a breath and dives
decades deep as the porpoise and her young one rise — submerge
— rise — submerge — through the surge of sea extending from cliff
to horizon. He locates

the echo
of another
feeling

too — and important though he recognises species monitoring to
be, he's got the urge to preserve this stirring of glee, conceal his
recording sheet, keep his sighting secret.

left
in their original
language

un-
translated
into data

there
they are / were —
look! —

on the tip
of his tongue
now

gone

Data Deficient

Necklace

Hippocampus hippocampus

Some rare, endangered Sundays, my mother
would let me unlatch her jewellery box
and pick one piece to wear. Didn't bother
with the gold, oval locket holding locks
of my balding father's hair, the red fox
brooch, or the bracelet with charms whose luck dried
up in The Drought: chose the shell with the shock
of the tiny seahorse confined inside.
Tried not to mind it had wrongfully died,
tried to believe I could rightfully hear
mermaids flirting, cod-song, waves of *Beside
the Seaside* when I pressed it to my ear.
Wearing it triggered an uneasy wish —
Please let me always feel free as a fish.

Remember

Hippocampus guttulatus

> *There was that time when*
> *Don't think I ever*
> *Who did you say we*

In the Atlantic of his mind,
thoughts once danced together daily,
advanced through dense strands of eelgrass,
dismissed the passivity of plankton.
And he could brood, then hatch,
a spiny batch of ideas overnight.

Now, though, age has cast
         its anchor.
Lone   thoughts   swim
in an unfathomed limbic sea.   Most get   snatched
from the fronds towhich theyattach
         to   stutter
   in   the   sun
on some cluttered foreignquay.

> *It was*

> *But I*

> *Something about a*

.

Near Threatened

Monstrous

Chlamydoselachus anguineus

because you're blatantly not Bambi *it sure ain't pretty* because you're
not feathered or furred *a freaky thing* because you've slithered
from fiction *quite horrific* risen from the deep sea serpent stories
we've heard because you're *like the chestburster in Alien* because the
fisherman who netted you off Gippsland must gestate his fear for
the next three-and-a-half years because even though we've tried to
tame you with a term reserved for skirts and curtains you remain
like nothing researchers have ever seen because of your *insane teeth*
three hundred tiny tridents because you're not iconic or marquee
dead-looking eyes because in spite of it being more than half your size,
when you distend your jaws, you readily ingest our tendency to
anthropomorphise because you predate our mammalian uprise by
eighty million years *straight from a nightmare* because we'd happily
let pandas claim your place in the ark *once you're in that mouth you're
not coming out* because you decided to die just hours after capture
the one time you were tanked in a marine park *poses no danger to
humans though scientists have accidentally cut themselves examining its
teeth* because you won't even meet our preconceptions of shark

Watch
Lutra lutra

I've learnt to not spot,
to disregard logs,
to track absence.

I've traced his prints —
my fingertips have kissed the space
where his paws nimbled
for an instant.

I've scooped and microscoped spraint,
grown intimate with his prey.
By counting the rings of its scales,
I've aged the trout he duskly ate.

Others' spraint I've left in place —
on rocks where waters web and knot,
in the underdark of bridges.
I've trained my nose to know
which is toaded with bones,
who's aching to mate, or cubbing.

I've switched to snacking on carp
and crayfish, un zipped
amphibian   skins, garnished
the grass with tail fins and jelly.

Now oaked among roots
                I can feel
the river dream him again.

        Quickslide
            down
                the bankside

        tarka my way
                            upstream

Watched
Prionace glauca

Always tagging. Always tracking.
Always cracking the wise
when you analyse our sexbiting.

Always viewing our lives
through a glass-bottomed heart.
Always ruing the part you've played

in our demise. Always bluing
the air. Always claiming there are twenty
million more to spare. Always saming

and saming. Always naming
a price for off-sliced fin. Always ticking
the box next to thicking of skin. Always

countershading. Always mounting
your panting pages of data. Always baiting
your breath with blamings and stats.

Always wording. Always herding
us into bar charts and grids.
Always blurting our secrets

of squid and awaying. Always saying
you're not. Always flossing the loss
from your teeth. Always sleeking

with relief that we're still here.

Vulnerable

Build
Physeter macrocephalus

There won't be a manual.
Don't expect instructions to be etched,
as scrimshaw, on a tooth.
Don't panic-flick through *Moby-Dick*.
Think benthic.

Begin with the insides.
Don't try to refine the design —
just bear in mind, as you loop
            and wind
    its quarter
                mile of intestines,
that you'll need to add an enzyme
which can form chyme from plastic.

Though you'll flail many times, waist-deep
in spermaceti, you must never fail
to grin. A frown
will rigidify collapsible ribs;
a curse could shift   blowhole
        to fin.

When straining to start its skiff-sized heart,
cling, like a giant squid, to your task,
till your will inflicts suction cup marks
on its rippling Pacific of skin.

Make sure you've got thrash metal blaring
as you fill it with clicks
            and breath
                on the off-chance
that this'll prepare it for decades of drilling
and seismic tests.

Be ready for the moment when it outknows you,
when the weight of its brain takes over
and goads you
to renovate yourself.

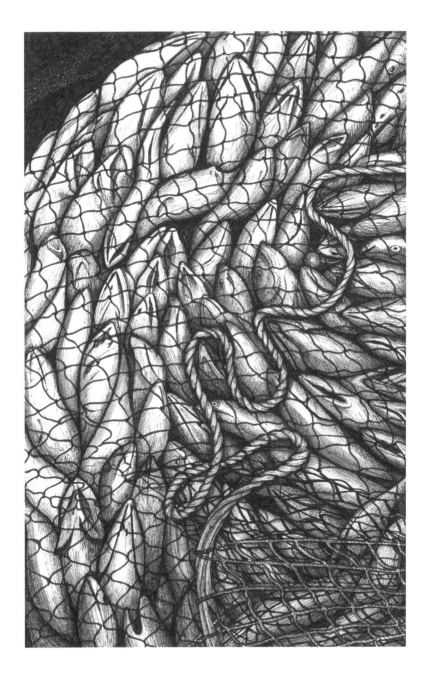

Song
Gadus morhua

Play me a demersal, non-commercial
song about cod.

Not the punk nursery rhyme —
Captain Birdseye sticking up
                    two frozen fingers
at the North Atlantic wars,
his mohawk spiked
with globs of parsley sauce.

And not the trance anthem
from the Grand Banks —
fishermen remixed
        into makers of bakeapple jam
and folk artists,
permitted to catch
only shoals of trippers and tourists.

Play me, instead,
a song that's barely heard —
so rare I must work, long-term,
to learn its three-part harmony
of fin displays and males inverting
                    themselves
beneath their mates,
each pair riffing
                    in rhapsodic circles.

Hound

Squalus acanthias

If we train her to *Wait!*, might she fail
to migrate and evade
all slavering trawlers?

Can we teach her to retrieve the past,
which used to   bounce   when we threw it,
before the deepest
                        plunge
in her numbers?

Will she learn to bury our bony blunders
in the mud of the sea floor
and will her back's toxic spines,
like hackles, rise,
when anyone tries to exhume them?

If we never say *Hey! Rock Salmon!* —
the alias we gave her for edible appeal —
will she feel more inclined to come to our side
when called?

If we refuse to believe we need to beautify her breed
(more endearing face, more expressive eyes),
will she never be demeaned
by the prize of Best In Show?

Might she fertilise our hearts when she dies?
Not hauled on a longline,
        but caudal fin   swishing   with the bliss
of being old.

Waste
Dermochelys coriacea

1. Net

The Ghost of Fishing Past has failed
        to fade.
It will haunt degradable dreams
for decade after leathery decade.

The Ghost of Fishing Present
is not the one doing the moaning.
What you hear is the sound
of a thousand gouged flippers.
Mangled skin. Tangled necks.
Flexible shells yelling for protection.

The Ghost of Fishing Yet to Come
nets every ocean current and tide.
Entire gyres are trapped.
Waves   writhe   and   thrash
as the sea sinks
                to the bottom of itself.

2. Bag

Her prey migrates
from chip shop
and Tesco
from High Street
and suburb from
windgust and
gutter from
fly-tip and
river from
storm drain
and foreshore
from shallows
and deeps
till it reaches
the pelagic zone,
her home
in the open sea.
As it floats
past, she grabs
it, drags it
down her
barbed throat,
adds it to
a gut already
stuffed with
polyethylene.

Meanwhile,
near to
the surface,
genuine jellyfish
themselves ingest
plastic plankton.

Unknown
Oxynotus centrina

I trawl for facts
but just grab a few as bycatch
while preoccupied with Cod.

I fish for myths but land just one —
if modern mariners,
under a mozzarella sun,
ever glimpse him,   they   flinch
and cross themselves,
       tongues tangled
              in overcooked
     strands of prayer.

I fashion a medieval map,
add him to the *Here Be's* and Sea Pigs,
wrap Leviathans round the ships
whose crews would construe
his commercial value.

I create a petition to change
his name, to untame it with adjectives
that don't describe edge and surface
but reveal the beneath and inside.

I campaign for Information Conservation Zones,
where knowing must be hooked,
     then released —
              alive.

Fantasy

Eunicella verrucosa

Your pink sea fantasy
should not include Neptune modelling thongweed,
or a school of mermaids spanking
zooplankton from their hair.
It should contain no selkie stripteasing her skin
or an octopus in fishnets (four pairs).

The seventh wave ought not misbehave
in your pink sea fantasy
or make of it an epic disaster flick,
the risen tide overswum
by giant, horny Gorgonians.

Instead, let cleaner wrasse arrive
to eat the lice from your pink sea fantasy
(heedless divers, dropped
            anchors,
the greed for souvenirs)

till you hear the moral in its branches —
how the catch got its by,
how the scallop found its dredge —
pursed, like catshark eggs,
in the soft of its coralling.

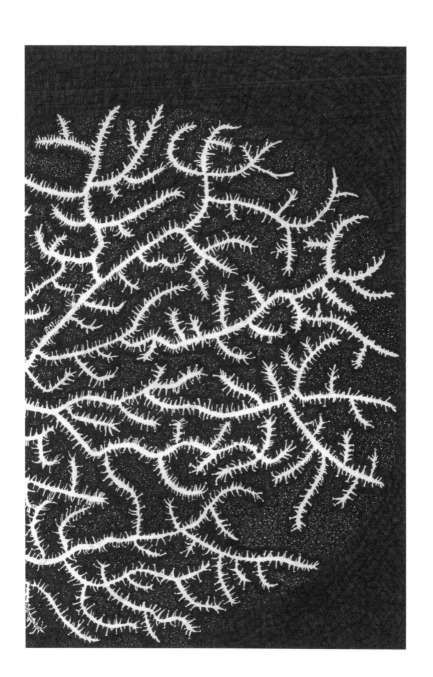

Bask

Cetorhinus maximus

He'd never been a guppy kind of guy,
happy with the love of insignificant fish,
with a string of trivial fry.

This time, fixed on the biggest prize,
he tiled his whole home from ceiling
to floor, installed a fathomless bath,
knocked through walls to enable the circling,
tripled the width of the front door.

His mates nicked his phone,
switched the ringtone to Jaws,
fake-bloodied the surf,
while his father prayed
for his lunate soul at church.

Too late, he came to realise she'd never stop gaping,
gulping whatever lay in her path —
plastic bags, bubble wrap, cushions and spoons,
takeaway cartons, curtains, his power tools,
microdoubts in their thousands,
his reputation for cool.

Now, he's changed all his passwords to squalene,
committed to start
craving to win her liver
in lieu of her heart.

Pledge
Alopias vulpinus

Let us craft carpets from marine debris.
Let us slough off
our styrofoam greed for bowls of fin soup,
using gritty insistence instead
of microbeads. Let us fix a filter
to our washing machines
to prevent our nanofibres reaching
the sea and begetting synthetic herring
and anchovies. Let us unlay
the cables that derange
your electroreceptors.
Let us fill gillnets
with nothing but the will to steeply increase
your numbers. Let us weep
no more mermaids' tears. Let us
leap clear of our pelagic fear
that it's too late to change.
Let us mount a campaign to unpurse
the seine. Let us generate and
maintain a higher internal purpose
than that of our surrounds. Let
us herd our diurnal urge for PVC
into a shoal and stun it
with one thrash of our faith
in your recovery. Let us prey
only on apathy.

Stench
Galeorhinus galeus

Imagine smelling more
than that drop of blood
          in the water
   a quarter of a mile away;
more than location, source,
and readiness for sex or eating.
Imagine smelling dolphins' one-eyed sleep,
sea stars' tube feet,
the hubris of scuba.
Imagine two nasal tracts,
       undistracted by breathing.
Imagine smelling the creeping acidity of sea,
    tiny shelled terrors,
chemical errors in the blood cells
of dab and pouting.
Imagine reading those smells
that are long out of print —
the origin of salt,
       oxygen's   historic drift,
          misspellings
of sinks
     of carbon.
Imagine smelling that urge
   to purge an estuary
of its role as a long-term nursery;
her internal   stilted   hatch   of eggs,
the silted stench
        of her last
    birthing.

Cartoon
Fratercula arctica

Easy to cleave to our cliché 'clown of the sea'
and believe he's Looney Tuning,
old-school cartooning, comical-waddling
on those Technicolor feet.

And easy to watch his foes, Misters Overtrawl
and Overheat, get thrust from the thrifty cliff
by his animated beak. See them hang
in mid-air, peek down, then thrash
and shriek *We'll get that pesky bird!*
        as they
                plummet
to their recovery.

Less easy, once he's burrowed, to accept
he's left the screen, to forgo
the fishy visual jokes,
to acquiesce to *That's All Folks!* plus the beat
       — not of stubby wings —
but Merrie Melodies.

Till, suddenly, this theme's drowned out —
his growly call from underground's like the electric sound
of a pencil being sharpened.

He's starting to sketch himself.

Play

Lamna nasus

love being on the cusp of tooth
      love quickswim and squidding
love egging little finniness —
         thousand egging

love best when frondling kelp
the overunder underover roll and oh
    the gilly tingle
not just skinridding   not just snailful
but wrap and tangle tag and   tug
      all feely with it
love sillying the timbers
love snouting the floaters till they   pop

better than sexscar
better than whiffs of flitting sleep
and better than their onesome funning —
the rippy throat   the   longlongstrung
then gutgash when they fin we   out
   in   thrash   of unsea above

Endangered

Create
Caretta caretta

In the beginning, she bore just barnacles
on her back, a hint of algae,
a hunch of Columbus crab.
Then, a succession of suckerfish attached
and as soon as each scute became a crucial habitat,
Man urged Coot and Muskrat to transfer to her
the whole murky balance of our world.

Centuries later, it should, she thinks, be lighter —
creatures uncreated, fuels burned —
and she ought to have earned the right
to make some other reptile take a turn
at carrying. But no — it's her carapace
that remains weighed down
by coastal developments,
industrial fishing gear, dubious intentions,
floodwalls bricked with fear.

She flippers with the idea of tipping it
          off her shell,
but the world won't be shifted.

As it glows and twists, lists
and groans, she can only spill
                    sea
from her eyes.

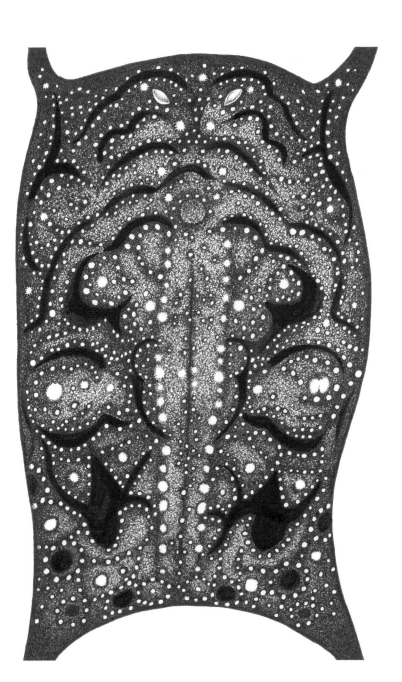

Purse

Raja undulata

This mermaid's purse holds no crab pincer comb,
no phone with a signature whistle ringtone,
no phosphorescence in a stick for glossing lips.
It won't be clutched at a shipwreck-chic cocktail do;
nor, in lieu of scallop shells, will it be used
to shield nipples from human view.
It holds, instead, the double-sided key to the future
of a species; the impulse to hatch, credit card-flat,
in roughly twelve weeks; the charged start of cartilage;
the faculty for forging forty rows of teeth.
Inside, too, is an aptitude for pattern — a swatch
of blots and Panadol dots to match the fabric
of the bottom of the sea. Most notably, it holds
the currency with which we'll pay
for our untold accidental catching,
our years of calculated greed.

Charmed

Balaenoptera borealis

She calls him from a thousand miles distance —
sends forth an invisible cord
from her edge of cliff

to his edge of existence.
She calls him in autumn storms,
in summer stillness,

grooves a new migration route,
moons him towards her
for tide after tide.

Some claim, with disdain,
that she practised with sprats; some beg
her to tame their cats

and mend their lame horses.
Others whisper that she's aiming
to become one, and hide

from her gaze, for upgrading
to rorqual takes whole shores of sorcery
compared with subsiding into seal.

She knows when he's close
from the tingle of krill on her tongue,
the pulse of his infrasonic hum

in her thighs, the unpleating
of her throat as she hazards a smile.
Though she's tiring, awed by his size,

she relies on no lyre to draw
him; no piping raises him, swaying,
from the waves. And when he finally arrives,

she defies the precipice, leans further,
further, further over the side, to tell
him why she fetched him, words stranding

between them like baleen:
Not to contrive more scientific lies,
not for those men rubbing krónur

from their eyes, but to show
that my kind need not be predators.
For no other reason but to see.

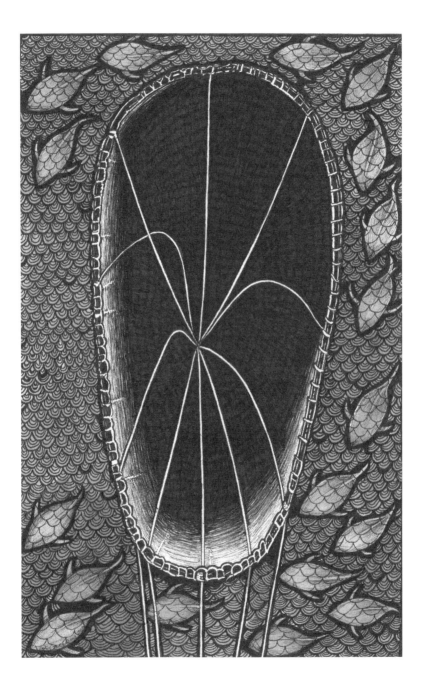

Wish

Thunnus thynnus

The sea shimmers with recognition,
          flexes   and   shifts, urged
by some dim, blue memory
to shrink as the fish surge forwards,
swell as they retract their fins.

Humpback whales sing the news
of the bumper numbers.
Dunes reverse their retreat.
Giant squid commute from the abyssal zone.
Sponge reefs soak up doubters' disbelief.

Hermit crabs turn extrovert as they hurtle
to spy the shoal, compass jellyfish guiding
the way. The tide can't stop itself rising
five times a day.

The moon refuses to move in its usual orbit — pursues,
and keeps beaming at,
the reintroduced. Ocean
          currents   reroute.
Skuas group into ticks of approval
across the swooping sky.

And men on a boat
no longer called *Sashimi*
          watch
without naming a price.

Augur

Melanitta fusca

A thousand in November
for a winter warm and wet.

One hundred for a tussle
in a double mussel bed.

Fifty for a westward
migrating coast.

Forty for a message
as plain as pigeon post.

Thirty for a nestward
expansion of mink.

Twenty for a hatchling
born not to swim but sink.

Ten for a tanker
lurching to the right.

Five for a wedge of wing
barred from being white.

Four, on the water,
for a shortage of fish.

Three for a dabble
in the shallows of a wish.

Two for a tomorrow
as hollow as the sky.

One for a lone hello.
None for a long goodbye.

Eye
Hippoglossus hippoglossus

sided-lop shift
optical drift
cross-skull nonplussing

    fresh angle of crab
    snatched curve of shrimp
    squinter than simple switch
    of gaze   astraying
    to full eye-dentity change

        now wowing
        at the right-above
        the two-times cod
        the double sculpin
        as I-socket halts
        and ossifies

            then itch of scales on the I-less side
            a twitch down the unpatterned lateral line
            at the think of what eye might
            be missing

                eye still remember
                the upright swim
                the lower jaw of the trawl net
                that terroring

                    though caudal fin flicks
                    with its northing frame of mind
                    the greatest migration begins
                    with the riddle of asymetry
                    ends with a sinistral sense
                    that gravel and sand
                    are also blind

Critically Endangered

Afterworld
Dipturus batis

Here, all animals are equal,
equal in extinction.

The Moa, long ago
an Is-No-More, dozes

with the Golden Toad;
the Aurochs shoulders

the load of the Great Auk.
The Quagga logs

all recent arrivals —
the Western Black Rhino,

shorn of her horn,
Lonesome George crawling

from the island of himself,
the Spix's Macaw clawing

at reports
of captive survivors.

The Pyrenean Ibex
takes vertiginous bets

on who's next —
the Caspian Tiger's

wild striped guess says
the Pygmy Three-Toed Sloth's

outpacing
himself, racing past

the red edge
of mangroves,

while dead glaciers wait
for the kiss

of the Snow Leopard's tread.
And look, here's

the Common Skate,
swimming against

the tide of her name,
cartilaginous kite

snarled in infinite
promises.

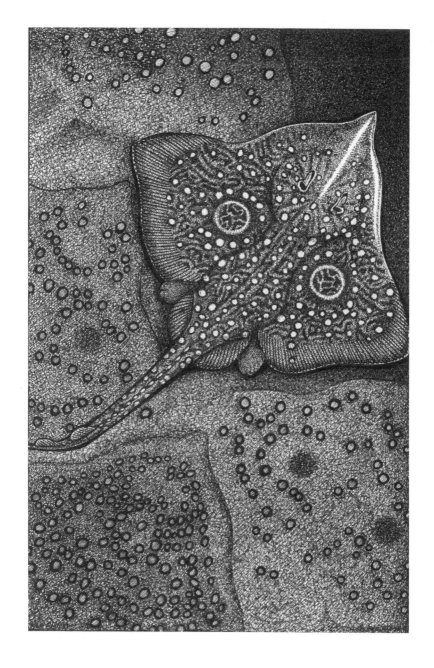

De-extinct
Squatina squatina

If we can inject an emptied egg
with DNA from a Pyrenean ibex

then embed it in a host domestic goat;
if we can tweak the genomes

of current cattle stocks
and strategically breed

till we've got an almost-aurochs;
if we can fashion fur and tusk

from mammoth cash;
fabricate great auks and engineer

sheer redemption —
we won't need to untrawl,

de-dredge, bid
bycatch bye-bye

for we can match
and mix, do

and un-die, get high
on tech, spawn sci-fact

from sci-fi, we can win
an extant grant

to forge pectoral fins like wings,
we can flatten its form,

pattern its back, gloss over
loss of habitat, install it

offshore, ignore
its first flawed ambush

of prey and say, *Yay!*
we can resurrect an angel.

Brink
Puffinus mauretanicus

It's the width of a gill slit of your prey away,
it's the fading of a flank from brown to grey away.
It's a take-off, from the sea, that's lacking strength away,
it's less than a longline's length away.
It's a cat with a nestling in its sights away,
it's a fledgling flummoxed by electric lights away.
It's the panting of a wave about to break away,
it's the catching of your mate (but by mistake) away.
It's a microplastic's shift from gut to blood away,
it's the comedown from a rave in a beachfront club away.
It's a chink in the storms that swarm from the west away,
it's a cloud on which the chin of the sun can rest away.
It's closer than the distance you migrate away,
it's weak resistance to the climate change debate away.
It's the rate your beak's twin nostrils excrete salt away,
it's a *sad to see but clearly not my fault* away.
It's new colonies of villas on the coast away,
it's an oiled, foiled wingbeat at most away.
It's a *sorry, I just haven't got the time* away,
it's the finding of a final line's end rhyme away.

glass
anguilla anguilla

through you
we can see
mudsuck moontug
the bore's gulp
and reach
thrust
of herons' beaks
scrinch and hulch
of crustaceans
through you
we can see
for ribboned miles
and weeks
far back as
the stipple
of salt
and sargasso
we can see
your epney ebb
magnified
the managed tide
sluice gates pumps
bankside tumps
occupied
by crooked rods
and lines
dark estuarine
netscoop
through you
we can see
no could-have-been
no slip
upstream
no freshwater
fleshing
no riverself slither
from
elver
to
silver

Plibble

Acipenser sturio

oshish soosh
oshish swosha
ish swossa sish sosh
ish sosh sish swossa
shosh oshish ishosh
ishla ishlash
soosha

shoshla oshibs
oshla-soobs sibs blish sooshla
slib sibs slissa blishlash issa-sibs
blosh sibs swobs libs sibla

balbib lib
libblebalbib
obibloob
ib ollabob obib
obib obla ob
obib bab ibble

Notes

Marine Conservation Information

The Marine Conservation Society (*www.mcsuk.org*) is a UK charity devoted to protecting ocean wildlife and tackling critical problems such as overfishing and plastic debris in order to restore healthy seas and shores. Its Thirty Threatened Species project highlights a range of marine creatures, all of whom appear on the IUCN (International Union for Conservation of Nature) Red List (*www.iucnredlist.org*). This list provides conservation status information on animals, plants and fungi worldwide, grouping them into such categories as Least Concern, Vulnerable, Endangered and Critically Endangered, and assessing which are most at risk of global extinction. The classification of each species is regularly reviewed and thus subject to change: the creatures who appear in this book are described according to their status at the time of my Marine Conservation Society residency.

More detailed information on each of the thirty species about whom I've written during the residency, as well as suggestions for action that can be taken to help them, can be found at: *www.mcsuk.org/30species*

'Plibble': Commentary and Translation

The linguistic, ecological and historical significance of 'Plibble' cannot be underestimated. Assumed to be the transcript of an elegiac utterance by the last sturgeon to be sighted in the Severn Estuary, in the vicinity of the village of Goldcliff, some three decades ago, it was discovered in the shed of fisherman Bob 'Hooker' Davis by his son following his death. There being no local speakers of Common Sturgeon remaining, the transcript was forthwith sent to leading authority Professor Véronique Dupont of the Université de la Garonne, initially to establish its veracity, and subsequently for detailed analysis and translation.

The most notable feature of Common Sturgeon, according to Professor Dupont, is its three distinct dialects — saltwater (see stanza 1, the consonant clusters of which echo the sound of the sea), freshwater (as exemplified in stanza 3, with its onomatopoeic riverine qualities) and estuarine (a transitional vernacular, as in the second stanza, which combines the sonic characteristics of the other two). Although it is believed that, as native speakers, sturgeon move freely between all three dialects from the age of twenty-four months, the language has unsurprisingly proved to be one of the most challenging in the Ichthyo family for humans to master, far more exacting than Atlantic Halibut or Cod, and exceeding even the complexities of Undulate Ray.

It is critical to recognise, too, another striking feature of 'Plibble' — the presence, throughout, of the first person singular pronoun ('ish' in the saltwater dialect, 'sibs' in estuarine and 'ib' in freshwater). It is rare for the first person singular pronoun to be used in an Ichthyo language — the first person plural pronoun, indicative of the individual fish's absorption into the shoal, is typically prevalent instead. Various theories for this anomaly have been expounded, ranging from the belief that the author of 'Plibble' had an uncommonly strong sense of self to the assertion that he or she was some kind of species patriarch/matriarch.

However, Professor Dupont argues that the use of the first person singular pronoun assuredly points to the fact that the last-known sturgeon in the Severn was in the throes of an acute existential crisis. He or she not only possessed a rare self-awareness, but also exhibited knowledge of his/her own — and, by definition, his/her whole species' — lonely impending end.

In the years since its discovery, 'Plibble' has been translated into a number of languages, including French, Welsh, English, Italian, Bulgarian, Romanian and Ukrainian, in acknowledgement of the sturgeon's historic range.

An attempt has been made, in the new translation that follows, to convey a flavour of the sonic contrasts in the three dialects of the original poem, and its form has also been retained. Punctuation has been added to aid clarity, which has occasioned some small modification to the rhythm, but no further literary liberties have been taken. The intention has been to provide a translation that cleaves to the original as closely as possible, presenting the voice of the sturgeon with the minimum of embellishment.

Gone

Acipenser sturio

Wistful sea.
Wishful sea.
I sought and swam,
swam and sought,
but the sea swarmed
with myself
alone.

Opposite of eel,[1]
I now lurch through the semi-sea[2],
not seeking to form self-likes[3],
but to keep searching for kin.

Thin water[4] soon.
Stopwater.[5]
Black taste.[6]
I'll breathe black.
Black outside.
Black in.

---

1. The author of 'Plibble' displays a prodigious level of awareness, not
   just of the life cycle of his/her own species, but also of that of a fellow
   critically endangered inhabitant of the salt- and freshwater ecosystems.
   Whereas sturgeon are born in freshwater, spend much of their lives at
   sea and return to their native rivers to spawn, European eels do the
   reverse, living in rivers and spawning at sea.
2. semi-sea (oshla-soobs) = estuary.
3. self-likes (issa-sibs) = offspring.
4. thin water (balbib) = freshwater/river.
5. In spite of the fact that Common Sturgeon is considered to be an ancient
   language that evolved little over the course of several millennia, it is
   thought that new terminology started to enter the lexicon at an unprec-
   edentedly rapid rate in the century prior to the creation of 'Plibble',
   doubtlessly reflecting the substantial adaptations the fish were being
   forced to make in their daily lives. Stopwater (libblebalbib) — in human
   parlance, constructions such as dams and weirs — is a perfect example
   of this trend.
6. black taste (obibloob) = pollution. This is another term to have entered
   the language comparatively recently.

Thirty Ways of Looking at the Sea

A tangle of smells — strands of salt, engine fuel and guano. Rise and fall of the boat — the sea's gentle intonation. Skim of oystercatchers, then the dying shrill of their cries. Sun on knees and the added warmth of my dog, Hooper, lying across sandalled feet. Backs of thighs sticking to the plastic cushion on the slatted seat.

Seeing the coast from this angle is both familiar and disorientating. I know every kink and ripple from the clifftop path but from sea level, the clefts and cracks and caves can't be readily recognised.

We bob past Craig yr Adar, which, true to its name of Birds Rock, would have been teeming with breeding guillemots and razorbills earlier in the summer. Now, it's a spacious perch for a few wing-drying cormorants and shags. Yet no-one on board seems concerned with watching birds, not even the tourist from Ohio with two cameras and a mammoth pair of binoculars slung round his neck.

The whitewashed former coastguard lookout shrinks to sugar cube-size as we continue onwards, southwestwards. Past the pebbled beach of Cwmtydu, which will become a grey seal pupping spot in a few weeks' time, requiring daily monitoring by volunteers to minimise disturbance from walkers, kayakers, dogs.

And on towards the tidal island of Ynys Lochtyn, its cliffs white-striped with quartz like droppings from a giant fulmar. Here, the skipper switches off the engine so the boat can idle for a short while. Activity on board intensifies, though, for bottlenose dolphins regularly feed in the waters off the island and this will be our best chance of spotting some. The researcher from Cardigan Bay Marine Wildlife Centre is on her feet, poised with pencil and clipboard to record dolphin data, and almost every passenger has binoculars pressed to eyes in the hope of spying a recurved dorsal fin among the bafflement of waves.

Nothing.

Ten minutes of fervent sea-scanning and nothing of note but four other tourist boats. Their presence is hardly surprising — back in New Quay, boat operators galore were plying their trade from harbourside kiosks or flaunting dolphin-emblazoned flyers along the path above the beach. One-hour, two-hour and four-hour trips. Romantic sunset trips. Each operator offering up to five a day. Though I live on the Pembrokeshire coast just an hour south of New Quay, I've never been on one of these trips before — overwhelmed, I finally chose the company that advertised the use of an underwater microphone with which we'd be able to listen to any dolphins we might meet.

By the end of another period of increasingly urgent searching, it's clear that the hydrophone's redundant today. 'Sorry, folks,' says the skipper, restarting the engine and swinging the boat back round in the direction of New Quay.

Cue disappointed sighs and groans. A child, clad head to toe in pink, hurls the cuddly dolphin she's been clutching across the deck and starts whining, as does her father. 'Meant to be a dolphin-watching trip. We promised Mia. We not gonna see any dolphins?'

I turn towards the cliffs again. Try to blank out the on-board whingeing by losing myself in the wind- and wave-sculpted faults and folds. Sea spray. Yellow lichen. Tumble of a glossy black bird. Fumble for a camera. Flash of red beak. Chough!

My close cliff-face focus attracts the man from Ohio over to my side of the boat. 'What d'ya see? Where is it?' His binos sweep wildly over every visible inch of sea and sky. 'Can't see anything. Where'd it go?'

Swoop of a herring gull, low over the boat. Swoop of Mia over Hooper. 'Can I stroke him?' she asks, prodding his left thigh.

Another gull, great black-backed this time. Ohio rolls his eyes. 'This trip's just gulls and water, man.'

As we chug and chunter our way back into New Quay harbour, I can see passengers for the three o'clock trip already queuing down the steps to the jetty.

'Sodding waste of money,' mutters Mia's dad as he lugs her, all snivels and flailing limbs, off the boat. And past the hopeful crowd.

'It's our thirtieth anniversary year and we're launching an appeal to help tackle the threats facing thirty marine species,' Debbie, the marketing manager of the Marine Conservation Society, has told me. 'They're all either resident in, or visitors to, UK waters and you'll find them all on the Red List produced by the International Union for Conservation of Nature.'

Debbie has driven to Wales from MCS HQ — which is located, rather ironically, in the landlocked county of Herefordshire — and we're in a café, deep in tea, cake and discussion. I've been passionately prattling about how I believe poetry can be a powerful tool in helping to raise awareness of the plight of endangered species and in encouraging people to work towards trying to save them. When I at last fall silent, I search Debbie's face for the look of bewilderment and/or panic that marketing managers of other organisations have sometimes assumed when I've tried to do the poetry hard-sell in the past, but she's beaming, gleaming-eyed. 'Let's talk about how we can get you involved in our Thirty Threatened Species project, then!'

I've specialised, as a poet, in wildlife conservation and other environmental concerns, for quite a few years now. Previous projects have included running writing workshops and penning new poems for Earth Hour, WWF's annual global lights-off event, as well as for Friends of the Earth's Bee Cause, a campaign for the permanent ban of pollinator-toxic pesticides. In the course of today's meeting, I learn that my involvement with MCS's Thirty Threatened Species project will be more long-term, a dream poetry residency for which an opportune chunk of funding has just become available. Over a second pot of tea, Debbie and I start to formulate what the residency will entail — as well as proposing to facilitate writing workshops to encourage others to engage with marine conservation, I gamely commit to the challenge of writing thirty poems myself, one for each of the endangered species.

Although, for the purpose of stimulating and sustaining public interest, MCS will reveal only one of the species on their website each week, I'm permitted to sneak a peek at the whole list. Reading it is an experience both exciting and daunting as I realise I have only sparse knowledge of the majority of the creatures about whom I'm being commissioned to write. Yes, some iconic marine mammals are included but many of the species live deep underwater, out of sight and inaccessible. I've only ever seen six of the creatures in the wild, plus the giant skeleton of another and a processed, breadcrumbed version of another on my school dinner plate in my pre-veggie childhood. And some of the creatures are now so rare, it seems, that there'll be little opportunity for me to see them in the future. No less than nine sharks are listed — how on earth will I produce nine sufficiently distinctive shark-themed poems? I will, it's clear, need to undertake some serious research and gain a broad range of practical experience in the months ahead. I'll need to speak to marine biologists and other experts, attend courses and conferences, and maybe do some volunteer sea monitoring work. Somehow, I'll need to compensate for the fact that my educational background is somewhat science-deficient and almost exclusively rooted in arts and languages too.

I have an imminent, and rather alarming, deadline by which to get my first couple of poems written, as the MCS AGM will shortly be taking place in Bristol. Aiming to attract several hundred attendees, it will, I'm told, be anything but a dry evening consisting solely of Apologies for Absence, Last Year's Minutes and Any Other Business. Instead, marine-themed talks relating to MCS projects will be delivered, writer and self-confessed whale-obsessive Philip Hoare, whose work I've long admired, will be speaking, and now a performance of my first couple of poems has been added to the programme too.

My choice of subject matter for the first of these poems is, thankfully, straightforward: I plump for one of the most familiar and accessible of the thirty species — the bottlenose dolphin. Our relationship with this creature is somewhat paradoxical. On the one hand, we permit thousands to die each year as fisheries bycatch; on the other, as I know from my recent New Quay boat trip experience, it's subject to an adulation that's bordering on the extreme. I recall my co-passengers' acute desire to set eyes on one, as well as their assumption that a pod would turn up on demand just like in a wildlife documentary. I also remember the simmering anger emanating from Mia's father when the dolphins failed to appear and the way in which he ultimately started bleating about wanting his money back.

A morning of internet research later and I'm ready to introduce other fetishistic aspects of our relationship with dolphins into my poem, provisionally titled 'Fluke'. Numerous worldwide swim-with-dolphins holidays are advertised, for example, promising euphoric connection and transformative healing experiences. How far, I mischievously speculate, might this infatuation take us? If we want to see dolphins so desperately and crave healing from them so urgently, might we start to manifest bottlenose dolphin tendencies ourselves?

For my second poem, I plunge out of my ripple-free comfort zone into choppier waters. Having written about one of the most familiar creatures from the Thirty Threatened Species list, I'm now going to persuade myself to engage with a life form with which I feel no immediate empathy and which actually looks more plant-like than animal. In fact, I realise that I currently think of the pink sea fan, a soft coral found off the coast of Wales and South West England, more as a threatened environment in which other creatures, such as sea slugs, live than as an endangered species in its own right.

As a route into the poem, and with the event at which I have to showcase it looming large in my mind, I decide to try to integrate some humour, even though the damage inflicted on sea fans from practices like scallop dredging and trawling inspires not laughter but despair. Yet since the AGM audience members will, I assume, be extremely knowledgeable about marine science and conservation, but perhaps not so enthusiastic about poetry, humour could be a way of winning them over, drawing them in. As I start to write 'Fantasy', I find that humour enables me to forge a connection with the pink sea fan too: it's the means by which I negotiate its strangeness.

Just wanted to tell you how much I admire your work... No. Too bland. Unoriginal.

I loved your whale talk earlier... Even worse.

'Leviathan' and 'The Sea Inside' are my favourite cetacean-themed works of non-fiction... No — too forced. Trying too hard.

The AGM has been a stimulating and convivial evening. I've enjoyed meeting, for the first time, some of MCS's marine scientists, and I'm relieved that poetry's centrality to tonight's event has been welcomed, rather than dismissed as a trivial adjunct to science. The audience has been warm and enthusiastic too and I feel thankful that my decision to try to weave some humour into my pink sea fan poem seems to have been vindicated. Now all that remains is for me to approach Philip Hoare and express some words of appreciation for his published writing without sounding too much like a burbling superfan. I especially want to respond to the enthralling talk he gave earlier in the evening about his long-term fascination with whales, and the remarkable journeys on which this fascination has taken him.

Your talk was so inspirational...

Too gushy by far.

In the days following the AGM, I start working on a poem about one of the whales on the Thirty Threatened Species list — the sperm whale — but do so with some trepidation. The subject feels so huge, not just in terms of its physical, but also in terms of its cultural, size, that I struggle to know where to start. Herman Melville's *Moby-Dick* surfaces at the forefront of my mind, as does the bloody centuries-long history of whale-hunting for spermaceti, the waxy substance created by an organ in the whale's head, that was used to make candles, cosmetics, pharmaceuticals. And I feel overawed by contemporary accounts of epiphanic encounters with sperm whales too, not least Philip Hoare's intimate underwater meeting with a matriarch who made eye contact with him and, with her sonar, 'read' his body from head to toe. How can I possibly hope to write anything meaningful or express any significant insights in comparison with that?

I'm aware that my only, comparatively trifling, contact with a sperm whale came some ten years ago while I was travelling on a writing fellowship through Newfoundland. I was heading up the island's Great Northern Peninsula, flanked by stunted spruce trees and beaches strewn with the rusty guts of a wrecked steamship. In need of provisions, I detoured into Port au Choix, a settlement located on a nub of land bulging into the Gulf of St. Lawrence, where, after stocking up in a Groceteria, I wandered into the Museum of Whales and Things.

It was a one-man, one-room, homespun clutter of a museum full of fishing nets, lobster pots, wading boots, live crabs in a Tidal Pool Touch Tank — and the dramatic centrepiece, the skeleton of a fourteen-metre-long sperm whale. On the handwritten explanation alongside it, I read that the creator of the museum, folk artist Ben Ploughman, felt impelled, a few years back, to spend several days defleshing a dead, stranded whale on the nearby shore. After burying the flesh, he boiled and bleached the fetid pile of bones in a vat made from an oil drum and then reassembled the skeleton. At the time of my visit, all the bones were labelled and suspended from the ceiling, clanking against each other like giant wind chimes. A final handwritten sign informed me that the whale skeleton was 'For Rent, October-April.'

My memory of Ben Ploughman's reconstruction of the skeleton is the unexpected stimulus for 'Build', the sperm whale poem that I eventually come to write, in which a list of instructions is offered, not just for the assembling of a skeleton, but for the manufacture of a new sperm whale entirely from scratch. And instead of directing us to fight to outlaw the threats that the sperm whale's facing (such as ocean plastics which the whale ingests, and the blasts that occur during seismic tests for oil and gas reserves which can cause neurotrauma and trigger strandings), the instructions recommend that we simply build a more adaptable sperm whale, one who's better equipped to deal with all the dangers.

At the same time as I'm assembling the bones of my sperm whale poem, I'm planning for the first of my Thirty Threatened Species writing workshops. It takes place — quite incongruously, given the wave-washed, briny subject matter — in the elegant dining room of a Georgian hotel in MCS's home county of Herefordshire. As is often the case when I run workshops for environmental organisations, the group that gathers is a diverse one, containing a mix of avid writers who aren't so familiar with the world of marine protection, and passionate conservationists, including several experienced scuba divers, who have little previous interest in writing poetry. I love working with groups of this kind, encouraging participants to swap knowledge and draw on each other's areas of expertise.

The theme of this particular workshop presents additional challenges. As I know from certain responses to my pre-workshop publicity, not everyone's going to be ready to focus exclusively on species loss and potential extinction.

'It sounds like it's going to be a bit depressing,' wrote one woman in an email, as she dithered over whether to book the remaining workshop place. 'I wish we could celebrate what's left and still abundant instead.'

I've got the task of making cold-blooded creatures, about whom people might not instinctively feel enthused, more accessible, too. As part of my preparation for the workshop, I introduced some of the Thirty Threatened Species to one of my ongoing writing groups to gauge what the reaction might be.

'I just can't get excited about fish.'

'Me neither.'

'Nor sharks. They're a bit sinister. Scary.'

'And some of those other creatures you talked about are really weird. Wouldn't know how to write about them at all.'

I've consequently come up with a few techniques that might encourage any reluctant Herefordshire workshop attendees to connect with, and care about the conservation of, the less immediately appealing threatened species. It might be possible to render the creatures more familiar in the actual process of writing, for example, by using domestic, human-focused similes and metaphors.

My other, more drastic, option is to eschew the pink sea fans and others of their ilk for at least one workshop session and concentrate on the creatures who are better known and loved instead. Given that my biggest challenge of all right now is to ensure that each participant produces a poem in the workshop environment that they're happy to take away, rework and practise reading in time for appearing at the Hay Festival Winter Weekend, at which an MCS Poetry in Ocean event has been programmed, in just over a month's time, this is a tempting route to take.

Irresistible, even. Tapping into some of the participants' memories of coastal holidays from childhood and beyond instantly sparks a lively pod of bottlenose dolphin poems.

Relief. We're underway.

For my own next poem, I tap into a childhood memory too.

Opening the bottom drawer of my mother's dressing table, struggling to lift out her wooden jewellery box, preserved for several decades from her 1950s youth. Sitting on the bedroom floor with it wedged between my white-socked legs, its plain exterior belying the gaudy promise of its insides.

Unlatching and raising the lid — slowly.

Initially, just looking. Then, dipping my fingers in, jangling them through the silver charm bracelet, the plastic fruity Carmen Miranda necklace, the clip-on flower earrings, the brooch in the shape of a fox with red crystals for eyes. Heart beating a little faster — where's my favourite necklace? Each time, half-expecting not to find it. Can't see it. Is it still here?

Yes! So well hidden! Buried under the long loops of mock pearls. Pull it out carefully, disentangle it from the locket chain.

Got it.

Rest the scallop shell in the palm of my hand. Finger its ridges. Hook the leather cord over my thumb, swing it gently back and forth. Back and forth.

And now, peep inside the shell. Again, half-fear it won't be there.

Expel a breath.

Of course it's there.

The tiny, brown, dried seahorse.

I adore all animals and am consistently drawn like a tuna to a bait ball to this item of jewellery. But, at the age of seven, I fail to make the connection between my love for animals and the fact that a rare marine creature has been harvested for the sake of creating a frivolous fashion accessory. If I were to have made the connection, I'd have been horrified. Or perhaps tried to make myself believe that the seahorse was so tiny compared to the picture in my animal encyclopedia that it couldn't possibly be real.

Although all the poems I've written thus far have been in free verse, the subject matter and the theme of entrapment that emerges demand a more rigid structure. 'Necklace', a short-snouted seahorse sonnet — rather a claustrophobic one, I hope — is the result.

After producing a somewhat oppressive poem centred on lifelessness and lack, I feel ready to revisit more expansive memories of a creature which, in spite of its appearance on the IUCN Red List, I still associate with profusion.

I've travelled to see puffins quite a number of times. I've stumbled in wind and relentless rain over a burrow-pocked cliff in Iceland, belly-crawled closer and closer to the edge, then bubbled, like a mudpot, with happiness on watching them land, striped beaks crammed with sand eels, on a ledge just below. I've lazed away a day on Westray in Orkney spotting puffins from a cliff warmed by sun and cushioned with pink thrift. And I've watched their stumpy-winged flight from sea to cliff with a mix of joy and unease on the Faroe Islands, aware that local tradition brings men out onto the crags with nets on sticks to hunt them.

For proximity to an epic number of birds, though, nothing compares to staying close to home and heading to Skomer Island off the west coast of Pembrokeshire in June or July. A visit at this peak breeding time, however, also means proximity to an epic number of humans. The first boat of the day leaves the tiny mainland harbour of Martin's Haven at 10 a.m., but many puffin-seekers, myself included on my most recent visit earlier in the year, queue from as early as 6, to be sure of securing one of the limited tickets.

Already, as we bump across Jack Sound, there's a flurry of puffins around the boat, beaks Belisha beacon-bright, wings beating to a blur. Others are hurtling towards their burrows in the cliff above Skomer's jetty, their presence mitigating our much slower, post-arrival slog up the steep steps to the top.

Pause to listen to the assistant warden's welcome talk. 'Keep to the marked footpaths... Don't block the puffins' access to their burrows... Compost toilets available in the old farm buildings...' Important info, but I've heard it many times before and am itching to walk on.

Follow the coast past the shrieking colony of kittiwakes.

Huddles of guillemots on the narrowest of ledges. At my feet, cruciforms of feather and bone, the remains of Manx shearwaters that have been preyed on by great black-backed gulls. Skomer supports what's said to be the most significant breeding population of Manxies in the world — more than 300,000 pairs.

And so to The Wick, a thin inlet and vertical cliff formed by geological fault activity, and the best seabird-watching spot on the island. With fish for their chicks silver-glinting in their beaks, puffins are flying in their hundreds from sea to land, disappearing into their burrows, re-emerging to preen, then winging out to sea again, the orange paddles of their feet splayed out behind them. In the face of such abundance, the puffin can't possibly be a threatened species. Surely.

A gang of nothing's-going-to-budge-us, camouflage-clad photographers arrives and claims prime, cliff-edge position. The whirring of their cameras as they fire off continuous shot after continuous shot echoes the puffins' throaty churring.

'Step back — let the puffin through!' a teacher calls to her group of primary school children. They bunch up against each other to create a gap, gasping and wowing as the bird waddles through to its burrow.

'Manners!' snaps a woman in flimsy, bird shit-streaked pumps. At first, I think she's irritated with one of the schoolkids, but then I realise that, bizarrely, she's addressing a puffin. It seems she stepped aside to let it pass but it barrelled on towards its burrow without stopping to thank her.

Seized by the need to grab a few minutes away from the crowds, I head up a grassy incline beyond the main cluster of burrows. Stop. Breathe. Look out to sea. On the horizon to the west is the island of Grassholm, home to the third-largest colony of gannets in the world, its humped form topped with white guano giving it the look of a classic Christmas pudding.

'Hallo! Very fine, this place!'

Damn. A man. Bushy beard for mumbling into and a German accent.

'Looney Tunes!' is what I think he says next.

I polite-smile and nod, assuming he's alluding to the puffins' cartoonish qualities. When he gestures towards Grassholm and the tumbling sea, though, it dawns on me that what he actually said was 'Lovely views!'

My memory of this minor misunderstanding ends up being the stimulus for my puffin poem. In it, I develop a series of cartoon-related images, while trying to express something of the overbearing nature of the puffin-watching process, to which I, too, have, of course, contributed. In the level of adulation they inspire, puffins are the avian equivalent of the bottlenose dolphin and only when they're in their burrows can they escape both the human gaze and the many clichés we impose on them.

As for my belief in puffin abundance, I'm not able to sustain it for long beyond my writing of 'Cartoon'. Thanks, in part, to the puffin's susceptibility to the effects of climate change, especially sea temperature rise which is causing the redistribution of its prey, its IUCN Red List category gets upgraded from Least Concern to Vulnerable.

It's two days until the Poetry in Ocean event at the Hay Festival Winter Weekend. I've been liaising closely with Dr. Peter Richardson, MCS's bespectacled, bearded biodiversity programme manager and turtle nerd: together, we'll be offering a blend of poetry and science themed around the Thirty Threatened Species project. Some of my workshoppers will be sharing their poetry too and, a few nerves aside, they're raring to step up on stage to read their well-honed and toned poems. I feel underprepared in comparison and need to get at least one more poem written to fill my allotted time.

I decide to try channelling some of the writing-at-the-last-minute energy I used to draw on during my stint as poet-in-residence on BBC Radio 4's Saturday Live. Over a four-year period, I was one of a small number of poets from different parts of the UK who'd be called in to Broadcasting House in London every couple of months to write and perform two new poems for the live show. The first poem, all of thirty seconds long, had to open the show and be themed around a top news story of the week, while poem number two, lasting for exactly a minute, needed to be written in response to one of the items featured during the programme. With such an absurdly tight deadline, there could be no hours spent agonising over the placement of a comma or any other preciousness surrounding the poetry-writing process. Once I'd moved through the blind panic stage, my usual solution was to produce a poem full of sound patterns — alliteration and assonance, a string of half-rhymes — and aim for a playfulness and inventiveness with language that would hopefully not only serve to distract listeners from the fact that the content was a bit thin but also raise a smile.

The Balearic shearwater poem, 'Brink', that I finally write just hours before our Winter Weekend event in Hay-on-Wye gets underway, follows a similar pattern. Brief, but intense, online research teaches me that the bird's closely related to, and slightly larger than, the Manx shearwaters I'm familiar with from Skomer but that its numbers are nowhere near as plentiful: it is, in fact, one of the rarest seabirds in the world and perilously close to extinction. I alight on a list structure for the poem, with each item in the list expressing, through a different image, the imminence of the bird's end, as well as some of the threats it's facing both at its Balearic breeding sites and in the wider ocean environment. To my surprise, in spite of the distressing subject matter and pressing deadline, I rather enjoy writing it.

I rather enjoy the Winter Weekend event too. Smaller and more intimate than the main Hay Festival that takes place in out-of-town marquees for ten days each May, the Winter Weekend's compressed into three days in late November. Poetry in Ocean's been allocated a room in the habitable part of crumbling, atmospheric Hay Castle and although we have an early Sunday morning slot that makes me doubtful of a big audience, I'm mightily chuffed with the number of people who come along.

'So, are you two related?' is the first question that Peter and I, sharing the same surname, are asked, post-performance, by a succession of audience members. Other, more consequential, questions soon follow, though, most notably about what practical steps individuals can take to help the marine species we've been speaking about.

'I loved learning all those facts about sharks and dolphins and whales,' says a lanky, stoop-shouldered lad who I'd assumed was texting during the event but who turned out to be using his phone to take notes. 'And the poems really made me, like, care about them a lot.'

The woman next to him nods. 'Reckon it's time to get online and find some petitions to sign.'

I feel grateful for this feedback: the event's helped to boost my belief that poetry has a vital role to play in encouraging engagement with marine wildlife conservation.

I'm grateful for the event for another reason too. Ever since I made a start on writing the thirty poems, I've been pondering on what overall structure the eventual collection should have. Should I group the poems according to species — reptiles/fish/birds/

mammals — for example? Or wait until I've finished writing them all and see if an order suggests itself, as when I shaped my previous collections? Thankfully, Peter's contribution to Poetry in Ocean provides me with the ideal narrative arc — he opened by speaking about the creatures whose IUCN Red List status is Least Concern, then moved through Data Deficient, Near Threatened, Vulnerable and Endangered, before ending with Critically Endangered, those marine creatures that are all but extinct.

And having heard him, it now seems essential, for maximum impact, to group the poems in the same way.

Having been so busy in the weeks leading up to the Winter Weekend — writing, helping to publicise the event, collaborating with Peter, mentoring the workshoppers — I'm ready to enjoy a few weeks that aren't quite so deadline-infused. Rather like the old adage that you wait ages for a bus and then two come along at once, however, I suddenly find myself with a second poetry residency to fulfil, this time with the international animal welfare initiative, World Animal Day.

With its mission of working to create, through education and consciousness-raising, a reality in which all creatures are recognised, across the planet, as sentient beings, World Animal Day is celebrated each year on October 4th. I'm thrilled to be involved, my task being to help generate awareness of, and support for, animal welfare in general and World Animal Day in particular, through the writing and performance of specially-commissioned poetry. Fortunately, this residency doesn't require me to write thirty poems in one fell swoop — rather, I'm to produce a maximum of two per year, one of which will always be unveiled and circulated on World Animal Day itself.

'Puppy farming! Animal experimentation! The global problem of stray animals!' Caroline, the enterprising campaign director, reels off a host of issues that will keep me overflowing with ideas for poems for a decade to come. 'Or feel free to write on any subject of your choice.'

By the end of my first day of writing, I realise that 'any subject of my choice' is leading me to craft a poem that manages to straddle both of my residencies. Its setting is an imagined afterworld which contains all the animals who've become extinct over the centuries as a result of destructive human activities, and into which, I speculate, countless currently endangered creatures will also pass if our damaging behaviour continues unchecked.

Strangely, though, for all my recent focus on marine species, only one makes an appearance in the afterworld I've envisioned. Because of the common skate's relatively late maturity and inability to repopulate quickly, it's especially vulnerable to overfishing and, like so many of the other Threatened Species on the MCS list, it's also caught unintentionally in trawl nets, then discarded, dying or dead. Yet the skate only swims into view at the very end of 'Afterworld': it seems I need to summon a whole throng of more obviously enchanting mammals and birds before I'm ready to introduce this one cold-blooded fish.

Six years ago, yet the memory glitters like yesterday. A deep blue day of easy seas and effortless skies. Sailing west from Mull with my partner, Russell, and Hooper the hound, to Staffa and the Treshnish Isles. Columns of basalt rocks like organ pipes. The temple of Fingal's Cave. Hooper burying his nose deep in the grass topping Staffa's cliffs, then hurling himself onto his back, head and hips twisting unrestrainedly from side to side. Russell suspecting he's found some smears of guano to roll in but I prefer to attribute it to sheer joy.

Arriving at Lunga, the largest of the Treshnish Isles. Scrambling and laughing and slipping over gutweed-smothered rocks from moored boat to land. A picnic of bread, apples and cheese at the seabird colony of Harp Rock. It's too late in the season for the breeding puffins but there are still kittiwakes galore and sun-squinting views of uninhabited islands and other seductive hunks of land.

And, most memorable of all, the hours at sea in-between. A posse of harbour porpoises. Grey seals, hauled out on rocks, lifting whiskered faces to check us out, pausing for a quick front flipper scratch, then flopping back to sleep. A gasp of a glimpse of an adult minke whale and her calf. We distinguish most of these species by fin shape and size but Hooper's differentiating them by smell, front paws up on the side of the boat, sniffing the air.

And finally, so close to the boat that I could reach over the edge to touch it, another creature, the distance between its huge dorsal and caudal fins the greatest we've seen by far. And there — another! And another! All of them leisurely swimming and filter-feeding. One short, sharp bark from Hooper as if he, too, can't fathom their vast size, and then he falls silent again, watching, like me, mesmerised.

When it comes to having to write a poem about the basking shark, my initial feeling is resistance, sparked by sorrow at finding it on the Thirty Threatened Species list in the first place. As with the puffin, I refuse to let myself believe in the severity of its plight. Yes, it's been exploited, killed for its flesh, fins and liver oil, but we saw several of them so easily, without even trying. If a species is threatened, spotting it surely demands more of a struggle, with multiple attempts ending in disappointment.

Later, while still battling to reconcile myself to the shark's Red List status, I consider trying to write a lyrical poem centred on my idyllic Scottish islands day, and revisit some of Kathleen Jamie's marine wildlife-watching poems from her award-winning collection, *The Tree House*, for inspiration. Lyricism, however, sinks out of sight, leaving surrealism to surge to the surface. The poem that emerges charts the beginning and end of a relationship between a basking shark and a man who endeavours to win her love, converts his home in order to accommodate her size but ultimately loses interest. 'Bask' encapsulates, I think, my concerns around our attitude to conservation — a cause may become temporarily fashionable and attract a flurry of public interest but not the long-term commitment that's required.

I've paddled in the shallows of loss for too long. I've pretended it isn't happening by focusing on the illusion of bumper puffin and basking shark numbers or kept it at bay by embracing surrealism or by producing poems that trigger a grin. If I'm going to do justice to my Thirty Threatened Species residency role, though, and properly honour the endangered creatures on the list, I'm going to have to tackle the loss theme head-on. I'm going to have to accept the feelings of anxiety, grief and despair that I know are just a fin's width away. It's time to suck in a breath and plunge deep.

Time, too, to fully acknowledge that quite considerable loss has been lingering in my life for several years now. Loss of my mother, of both Russell's parents and of three close friends: each death, whether sudden or protracted, harrowing in its own way. My father's loss of memory, not just of daily domestic details, but of so much happy history that he and I have shared. The loss of some of the certainties of my own body as I'm buffeted by the first waves of the perimenopause.

A therapist friend of mine speaks of the importance of trying to balance loss with abundance — by growing vegetables, for example, and by feeding, and enjoying the presence of, garden birds. It crosses my mind that writing poetry can be seen as an attempt to do this too — an attempt to create and forge a presence in the face of absence and decline.

'Unknown', the first poem I write with my new dedication to the loss theme in mind, focuses on the angular rough shark, a creature about whom relatively little is understood, yet who's still under threat of extinction — going, going, gone, as a result of our unsustainable fishing practices even before we've bothered to properly acquaint ourselves with it. We've given the shark a prosaic name that describes what it looks like — pointed head and fins, coarse scales covering its body — but otherwise our knowledge is quite limited. Losing a species we never fully realised we had strikes me as being an excruciatingly poignant kind of loss.

My next poem, about the second seahorse, the long-snouted, on the Threatened Species list is rather more personal. It's prompted by my discovery that part of the seahorse's scientific name, *hippocampus*, is also the name given to the section of the brain that's thought to be the centre of memory and emotion — because it's seahorse-shaped, it seems. I thus start drafting a poem that aims to be about both risks to the seahorse's survival, such as anchors dropped by pleasure crafts in its seagrass environment and the profligate manner in which it's harvested for the curio trade, and a person's loss of self in late old age. Once I begin writing about the twin losses of species and memory, I feel as if I'll never stop, and an early version of 'Remember' runs to nearly two hundred lines. The final version is thankfully much tighter, the emotion more understated and compressed.

Tea-drenched café hours spent talking with visual artist Pat Gregory, my long-standing collaborator, turn out to be very helpful in terms of processing some of my embryonic thoughts and rawest feelings around loss. Pat and I have worked together on both print publications and accompanying exhibitions in a range of different ways in the past, from the intense collaboration of *Where the Air is Rarefied*, our joint collection of poetry and linocut prints, when we developed our ideas around environmental and mythological themes relating to the Far North simultaneously, to our work on *skindancing*, when Pat produced a number of pen-and-ink illustrations in response to my completed manuscript. This time, our work together seems to be evolving into a mix of those two approaches. Thanks to my Marine Conservation Society residency, we have the ready-made theme of imperilled animals and thirty designated species to engage with, but it still feels as if there's plenty of space and opportunity for us to meet semi-regularly and co-operatively develop some ideas.

'I'm interested in exploring patterns,' Pat reveals during one of our early discussions. 'Patterns created by waves. Patterns on the seabed. Some of the threatened creatures' patterned bodies.' The repetitions and rhythms of patterns can, she feels, offer a reassuring regularity in times of uncertainty and grief over impending species loss. 'Beauty's important too,' she adds, suggesting that making art or writing poetry which might be considered beautiful, even when the subject matter itself is not, can be an act of defiance against the ugliness of human-induced extinction.

One of the creatures whom Pat is moved to illustrate is the Atlantic halibut, another overfished and bycatch-susceptible species. I'm likewise keen to write a poem that celebrates the remarkable characteristics of an animal who wouldn't usually be considered beautiful, or even anything at all other than tomorrow's dinner. The quality that I'm especially eager to highlight is the migration of the halibut's eye from one side of its head to the other while the fish is in its larval stage, part of its process of transformation into a flatfish. Once this metamorphosis is complete, the halibut swims on its left side, with both eyes located on the right half of its head, for the rest of its life. I decide to write the poem in the voice of the halibut, a voice which becomes more stable, from a grammatical point of view, as the eye settles and stills. With Pat's comments on patterns prominent in my mind, I give close attention to the shape of this poem too, and persuade the stanzas to migrate from left to right across the page, mirroring the shift of the halibut's eye.

My hunger to discover other means by which to defy, and fight back against, unchecked species loss is temporarily satisfied when I become aware of the launch of a new charity, Rewilding Britain. Founded by writer and activist George Monbiot, its ambitious mission is to reverse centuries of environmental destruction and work towards 'the mass restoration of ecosystems in Britain, on land and at sea', a crucial element of which will involve the reintroduction of missing species. Among the lynxes, wolves, wild boars and beavers who are championed on Rewilding Britain's website as being prime reintroduction candidates is a marine creature from my Thirty Threatened Species list — the bluefin tuna. Decades of excessive commercial fishing, fuelled by high consumer demand and escalating prices, especially in Japan, caused the tuna's numbers to plummet across its North Atlantic range and despite quotas and other conservation measures being put in place, illegal catching has continued.

In the light of this, Rewilding Britain's claim that tuna 'need only a reduction in fishing pressure to return in large numbers' to UK waters sounds a tad simplistic. Yet compared with the complex and radical procedures that would need to be undertaken to reintroduce wolves, for example, I can understand why the argument for tuna is expressed in this way. The sense of possibility and ease that's conveyed is actually very alluring, and although poems of joy have themselves been critically endangered of late, I now find myself visualising a future world where overfishing is over and out, and writing a poem, 'Wish', in which the whole of the ocean environment is celebrating the tuna's reintroduced abundance.

From reintroduction to de-extinction.

I begin to read widely on the latter, as I'm keen to explore, through my next poem, whether bringing extinct creatures back from the dead could be another realistic strategy for stalling species loss. I come across some scientists expressing their wholehearted support for proceeding with cutting-edge genetic engineering and other scientists and conservationists who are emphatically against doing so. I read accounts of attempts that have already been made to revive lost species — a Pyrenean ibex that survived for about seven minutes, having been born to a host Spanish goat before it succumbed to severe lung problems, and the Dutch Tauros Programme that's committed to selectively breeding and crossbreeding certain varieties of domestic cattle in order to try to regain the wild Eurasian aurochs. Some ventures seem preposterous in the extreme, such as the multi-million-dollar scheme to clone a woolly mammoth and home it in a Siberian nature reserve called Pleistocene Park. Though I try to approach de-extinction with an open mind, the more I read, the more uncomfortable I feel about the processes involved and the implications for animal welfare. Disturbed, too, by the realisation that if we begin to believe that extinction's not 'forever' and there's always a chance that endangered species can be brought back at some later stage, we'll surely be less bothered about trying to save them in the first place.

The possibility of cloning a shark, has not, as far as I can gather, been mooted yet, but if scientific hubris ever moves us in that direction, the creature I choose as the focus of my poem — the broad-finned, flat-bodied angel shark — could be deemed to be the most in need. Because the angel shark buries itself in the sand or mud of the seabed in order to ambush its prey, benthic trawling has had a calamitous effect on its numbers. Shockingly, although it's clinging on as critically endangered in some areas, the angel shark is one creature on the Thirty Threatened Species list that has already, in its North Sea range at least, been declared extinct.

One shoe insole.
A nail brush.
A squeegee.
One sock.
Eight single-use carrier bags.
Six Diet Coke cans.
Five water bottles (two Evian, three Highland Spring).
Nylon fishing line.
A chunk of bucket.
Twelve cotton bud sticks.
An empty pouch of turkey-in-gravy Whiskas.
Seventy-two fragments of plastic.

I'm on my local beach in Pembrokeshire, with an ever-expanding black bin liner in one hand and a litter-picker like a giant pair of tongs in the other. High tide was barely an hour ago and the wet sand coating, and filling, some of the washed-up objects I've collected is making the bin liner increasingly heavy to carry, but at least the prevailing southwesterly wind can no longer tug it, as when it was in its flimsy empty state, out of my grasp. Unexpectedly, a large mastiff, who would ordinarily deposit a tennis ball at my feet and saliva down the front of my fleece, has today galloped towards me, barking ('Bruce just can't work out what you're doing.'). A man in green wellies and a wax jacket, meanwhile, has paused, hands behind his back, to offer advice — 'You've missed something — look! A balloon. Over there! Rubber.

Does that count?'

I'm here because ocean debris is my new obsession. And because I've been revisiting deep ecologist Joanna Macy's work on transforming denial, grief and despair around loss and the current planetary crisis into social and environmental activism. Earlier in the month, I embarked, along with thousands of others around the world, on a Massive Open Online Course (MOOC) on Marine Litter, run jointly by the United Nations Environment Programme and the Open University of the Netherlands. Although we're only two weeks into the course, I've come to realise that the scale of the ocean debris problem is even worse than I suspected — it's believed that almost every North Sea seabird now has plastic of some kind in its gut, for example. I've increasingly been feeling the need to do something constructive and practical, like regular beach cleans, to help tackle the problem, but I haven't yet started tackling a marine litter-themed poem. Since starting the course and taking on board the immensity of the issue, I've been veering between my usual evangelical belief in poetry's potential to make a difference, to inspire shifts in perception and create new patterns of thought and experience, and the fear that it changes nothing.

A toothbrush.
Three yoghurt pots.
A pair of red underpants.
One-third of a laundry basket.
Four disposable lighters.
Twenty-two bottle tops.
One strappy sandal decorated with plastic shells.
A length of thick blue rope.
A traffic cone.

Today, I'm skirting the edge of the dunes, yanking objects out of the sand and marram grass. It's so windy that I initially have to weigh down the bin liner with driftwood to limit the billowing. This time, it's a Yorkshire terrier who seems bemused by my stick-and-sack look, hurtling across the beach to yap around my ankles ('Oi! Monty! Come here! She'll put *you* in that rubbish bag if you're not careful.') while three other people feel obliged to bring me a rubber glove, a section of drainpipe and a plastic fork to add to my haul.

As I settle into my litter-picking rhythm, I think about the next Thirty Threatened Species poem that's finally starting to take shape in my head. There's evidence in my bin bag and all around me on the beach of two of the most significant marine litter threats: the presence both of pieces of plastic that creatures ingest, and abandoned rope and fishing line, known as ghost gear, in which animals become irrevocably entangled. The leatherback turtle is just one of the species that's suffering — as far as ingestion goes, it mistakes plastic bags for its usual jellyfish prey, its digestive system gets blocked and it ends up starving to death. It also becomes tangled in ghost gear and because of these two separate, yet related, perils, I've decided that 'Waste' will be a two-part poem. In the first part, I'm going to recast the Ghosts of Christmas Past, Present and Yet to Come from Dickens' *A Christmas Carol*, while in the second I'll follow the journey of a single-use plastic bag from Tesco to turtle gut.

Three sandwich cartons.
One mangled packet of sweet chilli crisps.
Six takeaway coffee cups.
Eight lids.
Two plastic stirrers.
A Bounty wrapper.
Three empty packs of fags.
Five dog poo bags — one empty, four full.

The composition of the debris is evolving as winter transitions into spring — almost everything I'm collecting today has, I suspect, been dropped by visitors to the beach. There are no large items like laundry baskets and drainpipes brought in on a storm tide.

My clothing and litter-picking accessories are evolving too. I'm wearing a fluorescent yellow hi-vis waistcoat and rather than carrying a generic black bin bag, I now have a bright red heavy-duty sack emblazoned with a Keep Wales Tidy logo. I met with Mari, Project Officer with Keep Wales Tidy, for an induction session earlier today and am on my way to becoming a KWT Litter Champ. As well as carrying out regular beach cleans, I have to do my best to spread the beach-cleaning word on social media and also chat about it to any members of the public who happen to be passing by.

Today, it seems, members of the public need no encouragement from me to start chatting. A man in a Help for Heroes sweatshirt waves, gives me a double thumbs-ups and bellows down from the car park above the beach — 'You're doing a great job! I mean it! I'd love to be able to help you! A *great* job!', while another man bustles up, all pink cheeks and frisky moustache — 'It's *so* nice to meet a fellow litter-picker. I'm part of the Civic Society in my hometown. We go out litter-picking twice a week.' Even the dogs I encounter seem more sociable now that I'm in my official Keep Wales Tidy garb — a pug plants her front paws halfway up my shins, then rolls over on her back for a tickle, while a sea-soaked golden retriever drops a plastic bottle on the sand in front of me and wags her tail expectantly until I snatch it up, decline to throw it and litter-pick it into my sack instead.

Half a Bic biro.
One empty bottle of Vet Lube.
Six fractured straws.
Two flip flops (not a pair).
Nine Quality Street wrappers.
Particles — too many to count — of blue plastic.
Numerous splinters of red.
Umpteen shards of green.

I've just completed Week Eight of the ocean debris MOOC and, as the sea mist slinks in and I painstakingly try to grab the tiniest slivers of litter from the sand with the chunky rubber jaws of my giant tongs, I wonder, for the zillionth time, what it will take to wean us off our addiction to plastic. I've been feeling particularly concerned about microplastics that enter the oceanic food chain and, due to the toxic chemicals they contain, disrupt organisms' reproductive and endocrine systems, with especially dangerous cumulative implications for those at the top of the chain. Thankfully, though, in addition to feeding my concern, the course has led me to learn about a host of inspirational anti-plastics projects that are being developed in many different areas of the world. These include campaigns for legislation against microbeads in beauty products, the creation of carpet tiles and school bags from washed-up rubbish, and the designing of filters for washing machines that trap synthetic microfibres which otherwise find their way into the ocean because they're too small to be detained in the wastewater treatment process.

The second of my marine litter poems, then, is going to be a call to arms. It will acknowledge the horror of our having damaged the planet to such an extent that the oceans will soon contain more plastics than fish, but it will move on from simply describing the scale of the problem: this new poem will insist that we still need to rise up and fight. And my rallying cry will, in part, be expressed through metaphors relating to the biology and behaviour of the thresher shark. Vulnerable to the all-too-familiar threats of bottom trawling, unmanaged longline and gillnet fishing, as well as plastic debris, the thresher shark has a remarkably long tail with which it thrashes, stuns and kills its prey. I'm a mite fearful that the poem will thrash, stun and kill its readers as 'Pledge' is the most obviously didactic Thirty Threatened Species poem I've produced. But I'm also feeling so inflamed by the urgency of the situation that I can't currently countenance writing in any other way.

A tideline of bladderwrack snarled in shreds of fishing net.
Two ice cream tubs.
The snapped-off handle of a child's beach spade.
Four lolly sticks.
A green Croc.
Sixty-eight cigarette butts.
A wedge of polystyrene.
One comb lacking twelve teeth.
A tracksuited man who does his best to peer inside my rubbish sack. 'Found anything useful? No? Oh well, keep looking.'
A tall woman in a long flapping mac, with white hair wisping from her bun. 'Bravo! Well done, girl!'

On one solitary occasion, I try to disassociate myself from all the litter and focus on the natural objects that the tide's delivered to the beach instead. Initially, everything I find seems to echo an item of waste in some way — common whelk eggcases like bubble wrap, fronds of red seaweed like limp balloons. The longer I spend fossicking, though, the more I start to see each object as it really is again without any reference to human debris. I rub my thumbs over the ribbed surface of cockleshells. Slip periwinkle shells into my pocket. Manipulate each brittle limb of the moulted exoskeletons of shore crabs. And untangle from clumps of spiral wrack the dark, leathery eggcases of sharks, skates and rays.

Without my Illustrated Guide to the Seashore and a bucket in which to do a few hours' worth of eggcase rehydration, I haven't got much hope of knowing to which species each belongs. There are subtle differences in size, shape and texture, as well as in the length of the horn-like forms extending from each corner of the eggcases, so at this stage I can't say whether any of them was produced by the endangered undulate ray. But one thing I do know is that all eggcases of this kind are widely referred to as 'mermaid's purses' and this feels like a potentially fertile starting point for an undulate ray-themed piece of writing.

As I wander along the beach, I find that I'm fossicking now through my brain for ideas for this new poem, rather than through the treasures of the tideline.

Will it be possible for me to develop the concept of what a mermaid might, or might not, carry in her handbag, while simultaneously revealing both the overexploitation the undulate ray suffers and information about its anatomy and habitat?

And will I also be able to convey a flavour of the fish's undulating movements — the way it ripples from its snout all along the edge of its disc-shaped body and wing-like pectoral fins — in the layout of 'Purse' on the page?

My own undulating movements, meanwhile, are ongoing: I'm still veering between a gung-ho belief in poetry's suitability for promoting environmental activism and a suspicion that it's ultimately ineffective and shouldn't even have an agenda in the first place.

Happily, I have the opportunity to explore my uncertainties at a day conference organised by the Centre for Human Animal Studies at Edge Hill University in Lancashire. The conference brings together academics and activists to examine 'how rethinking our relations with animals can create meaningful social, policy, environmental, ethical and cultural change'. I'm pleased to be contributing a presentation about poetry's role in consciousness-raising and inspiring behaviour change around marine wildlife conservation, as well as sharing some of my Thirty Threatened Species poems.

'Poetry's a powerful tool because in addition to, or even often instead of, engaging the intellect, it aims to engage the heart,' I begin, when the time arrives for me to take up position at the front of the lecture hall. 'And once someone's made an emotional connection with a particular issue, that connection's likely to be strong and enduring.' I cite action that some of my workshop participants have taken since they started to write poetry about endangered ocean species — many have switched to eating only certified sustainable seafood, several are badgering MPs about introducing a plastic bottle deposit return scheme, and one has committed to trying to live her life completely free of single-use plastics. But these acts are all on the micro-level, of course

— radical policy change is also what's needed. Ocean ecologists have long been calling for 30% of Britain's seas to be safeguarded from commercial exploitation, yet the reality is that only a fraction of 1% is currently protected from all forms of human disturbance. To what extent can poetry ever hope to change that?

In sharing some of the Thirty Threatened Species poems, I outline other challenges with which I'm grappling too. 'How possible is it to balance the urge to express an ecological message with the reluctance to be overly strident, which can alienate the reader?' I ask, referencing my recent experience of writing about the thresher shark. 'And what about when I'm commissioned to write an issue-specific poem, and need both to fulfil the brief and make the work accessible so as to reach the widest possible audience? Will the poetry I produce be of a quality with which I'm satisfied or will craft and technique be compromised at times?'

Though I leave the conference still undulating, still devoid of definitive answers, it's hugely helpful to discuss some of my thoughts with like-minded colleagues. Most gladdening of all, Jonathan Balcombe, an ethologist whose work I've long revered, is one of the keynote speakers, offering a lecture based on the book he's in the process of writing, *What A Fish Knows*, about the emotional and social lives of 'our underwater cousins'. I count myself very lucky to enjoy a stirring conversation with him once the conference draws to a close.

As the door of the first cubicle is opened, a grey-and-black-mottled common seal pup struggles to raise his head to look at me. His breathing is laboured and wheezy, as a result of the lungworm from which I've been told he's suffering. The temptation to croon soothing words in the sort of tone that I use on Hooper — 'It's okay, little one, you're going to be fine. Aren't you a beautiful boy!' — is overwhelming but I'm quickly warned against doing so by Alison, my quietly authoritative guide for the day. 'We don't talk to them and we try not to make eye contact. We don't want them to imprint on us. We need to keep them wild.'

I'm used to watching Atlantic grey seals around the coast of Pembrokeshire and have learnt a lot about them over the years. They're larger and comparatively robust: in fact, they're often referred to as being dog-like in contrast with the common or harbour seal's more delicate, cat-like appearance. I feel that I could dash off a whole sequence of grey seal poems without having to do any further research at all. But I know relatively little about the common seal, the species whose numbers have plummeted in recent decades, who is consequently on the IUCN Red List and about whom I have to write a Thirty Threatened Species poem, so I've travelled across the country to the RSPCA Wildlife Centre at East Winch in Norfolk to find out more about them and the struggles they face. The Centre originated as an emergency assessment unit in a disused bus shelter in 1988 when the RSPCA responded to the distemper epidemic that was causing the deaths of so many common seals in the North Sea and it's since become renowned for its care of sick, abandoned and injured pups and occasional adults. Having zipped myself into sterile white overalls, dragged on oversized wellies and waddled into the cubicle-lined critical care area, I'm feeling as ungainly as a seal out of water myself, but soon forget my discomfort as fascination with what Centre Manager Alison is telling me takes hold.

'He's got really harsh respiration — you can hear it,' she says as we watch the pup's body rise and fall. 'He's on all sorts of drugs to help him breathe, to help him open his airwaves. And we also steam him twice a day — turn off the ventilation and let some steam in to make him feel more comfortable.'

I again bite back the urge to do cooing baby animals talk and ask Alison what she feels the prognosis is for the UK's population of common seals instead.

'Well, this year's been awful for commons,' she tells me sadly. 'They're immunosuppressed — they're really not a well bunch of seals. And we're due another distemper outbreak. I think it's going to be next year. I'm preparing for it mentally. Next year, we're due.'

After peeping into several other cubicles containing another sickly common seal pup, a few recently-rescued greys and an otter cub retrieved from an industrial estate far from any water course, I swap one set of disinfected wellies for another as I'm led by Alison out of the critical care area and into an adjacent seventeenth century barn.

'Everyone said, 'You should make this the Visitor Centre!'' she reveals with a chuckle, gesturing around at the vast space and high, beamed ceiling. 'But it's perfect for the seals. We don't need to heat it — it's warm in winter because of the thick walls, and cool in summer. It's lovely for them.'

I can't think of a better use for a four-hundred-year-old listed building either. The barn contains a row of fenced-off shallow pools in which segregated pairs of common and grey seal pups are continuing their rehabilitation. Compared with the limp, poorly creatures I've just seen in critical care, these pups are alert and more active. 'These guys are all self-feeding. Up to 800 grams of fish three times a day,' Alison explains, pausing to slit open a sack of salt which she tips into a pool occupied by a solitary common seal to help heal his sore eye. There's the hint of a quiver of emotion in her voice when she adds, 'Moving them out here and seeing them look so much better — it's what it's all about.'

Before their release back into the wild, the seals are nurtured through a final stage of recovery, transitioning into one of the larger, deeper pools in an outside courtyard. 'We feed them at random times so they don't know when it's coming and we feed them random amounts at this stage too,' Alison says, outlining the importance of replicating, as closely as possible, the unpredictability of food supplies that the pups will face at sea.

Though it would have been uplifting to head off from East Winch with the memory of a soon-to-be-released common seal pup swimming and playing in the fast-flowing water spouting from the recirculation pipe in her pool, the final image I'm left with is far more sobering. Alison shows me to a pool inhabited by an adult seal with a long, deep wound, a startling strip of pink, visible through the fur on the back of her neck. When she was admitted to East Winch, she was 'necklaced' — entangled in fishing net — and so unwell that Alison was convinced she would imminently die.

We talk a lot about wounds as we wend our way back along the Centre's maze of corridors to reception, and once I've signed out as a visitor, we linger at the exit, speaking about wounds some more. Entanglement wounds. Propeller and other boat injury wounds. Head wounds from shootings by fish farmers irritated at their salmon getting eaten and by fishermen who believe that seals are decimating 'their' stocks of cod. In spite of the inspiring and compassionate care offered by Alison, her staff and volunteers to help heal individual common seals, what long-term hope can there possibly be for the resurgence of the species as a whole when, in addition to the viruses and infections to which they're susceptible, there's a whole slew of human-induced threats to which they're regularly exposed?

While I draft and craft my common seal poem, 'Scar', I once again catch myself questioning the efficacy of writing wildlife conservation poetry, at least when compared with performing critical animal rescue and welfare work. Yet it still feels necessary to try to translate the common seal's adversity into words in the hope of bringing it to wider attention, and even though the subject matter's harrowing, it proves to be an easier poem to write than many. I figure that this is, in part, due to the fact that the common seal's an appealing mammal with expressive eyes, a creature with whom it feels natural to identify and for whom, as I well know from my visit to East Winch, sympathy's instantly elicited.

Stiffer writing challenges lie ahead. I'm now well over halfway through my Thirty Threatened Species list, yet there are still five shark poems with which I need to get to grips. Notwithstanding my evolving knowledge of ocean life, I'm continuing to find this a daunting prospect as I have no obvious route into the poems, no tangible means of connecting with any of the species.

In doing some preliminary reading about the porbeagle shark, however, I discover a trait that's gratefully embraced by my mammalian brain. Known first and foremost for being grossly overhunted for its meat, liver oil and fins, the porbeagle has also been observed exhibiting behaviour more popularly associated with primates, dogs, cats and the young of other iconic animals. The porbeagle shark readily engages in play.

I start to jot down a few lines in the voice of the porbeagle, and realise that the theme of play liberates me to be playful with language. Parts of speech begin to shapeshift: by the end of the first stanza, nouns are failing to always behave as nouns, and verbs as verbs, and there's no first person pronoun. My hope, as I continue to work on the poem, is that if the porbeagle is seen as a playful — and therefore closer-to-human — creature, rather than as something demonic, as is often the case with sharks, people may feel more troubled by the overexploitation it suffers and more moved to campaign to improve its vulnerable status.

The spiny dogfish is another shark species in the Vulnerable category about whom I need to write, and I get underway by doing some research into why it acquired its dogfish name. Although, in the process, I come across plenty of poem-pertinent general information — the fact that it still appears as rock salmon on chip shop menus despite there being regulations prohibiting it from being commercially harvested, for example, as well as its use in both pet food and fertiliser — I'm not able to track down a conclusive name-origin explanation. The way in which it shoals in dense doggish packs (incidentally making it extra-susceptible to being killed in large numbers as bycatch) is one, not greatly convincing, interpretation. All this dogfish name-pondering, though, does set me thinking about whether it might be possible to structure my poem around an extended canine metaphor, with 'Hound' as the title. By endowing the shark with recognisably canine characteristics, thereby domesticating a creature that seems very distant from our human realm of experience, I again hope to help generate both concern for its chronic decline and calls for it to be conserved with more urgency.

'Snakes occupy an uneasy place in human cultures, sometimes vilified for the fear and revulsion they evoke and also killed for their skin or as perceived threats,' says Professor Emily Brady at the start of her keynote lecture on 'Herpetological Beauty'. Since they're 'so unlike our own species', as well as furless, featherless and far removed from our favoured charismatic creatures, snakes 'can be difficult to engage with through sympathy or empathy' and we 'can't comfortably anthropomorphise them' either. Though Brady is lecturing on aesthetic engagement with snakes, all of her comments are, of course, eminently relevant to my experience of writing about sharks.

I'm at 'Cold Blood(ed): Enquiries into the Oddly Unloved', the latest conference of the British Animal Studies Network, which is convening, on this occasion, at Cardiff University. It's the first time I've been to one of the Network's meetings and I'm finding it very stimulating, not least because Animal Studies as an academic discipline is so wide-ranging, drawing together historians, geographers, artists, writers, sociologists and vets. Later in the day, I'm giving a presentation, 'Writing in Cold Blood', which will offer an overview of my Marine Conservation Society residency role, with emphasis on the fact that two-thirds of the creatures on the Thirty Threatened Species list are cold-blooded reptiles and fish. I plan to discuss some of the issues that have arisen while writing about, and coaxing others to write about, these 'oddly unloved' animals and will also perform a selection of my poems. I intend, too, to reference the poetry workshops I've previously devised for both WWF and Friends of the Earth's Bee Cause, to explore how fostering fascination with land mammals and social insects differed from my current fish-and-reptile experience.

First, though, I'm listening to, and am absorbed in the PowerPoint slides of, another paper, delivered by Art History

PhD candidate Sarah Wade, an analysis of two recent shark-themed art exhibitions at the Oceanographic Museum of Monaco. Acknowledging the exhibitions' 'overtly political aim of promoting shark conservation', she speaks of ways in which visitors were encouraged to reimagine their relationship with sharks through viewing work that sought to breed familiarity, evoke empathy and dispel ruthless man-eater myths. But, Wade argues, there's an alternative path for museums and galleries to follow. Trying to tame and modify sharks' wildness and strangeness through the use of domestic visual imagery (a practice that I recently adopted in my spiny dogfish poem, of course, and also urged my first workshop group to follow) is one option. But creating a sense of 'wonder based on difference' and focusing on sharks' ability to exude 'a non-human charisma' can inspire in visitors the desire to commit to conserving them too.

When I come to deliver my own presentation, half of my brain is focused on performing, while the other half is already preoccupied with how I can integrate some of the ideas that have emerged from the papers I've heard into my next poems. The deep-sea-dwelling, serpent-like frilled shark, with its three hundred teeth and distensible jaws that enable it to swallow prey over half its size, is arguably the least immediately appealing, and least seen, creature on the Thirty Threatened Species list. But this time, I won't try to tame it by alighting on some aspect of its behaviour that parallels the human or make it more attractive through the use of domestic imagery. Instead, the poem I produce post-conference will directly confront our inability to feel compassion or affection for a creature who's so different from ourselves. Throughout 'Monstrous', I'll highlight some of the sensationalist and negative language that was used in TV news reports when a frilled shark was netted off Japan in 2007 and off Australia in 2015. And I'll interweave verbatim quotes by Australian fishermen, reporters and news anchors with my own thoughts on our propensity to malign an 'ugly' creature who's so remote from us both physically and geographically, yet who poses no danger to us at all.

I'm eager to explore the notion of 'wonder based on difference' too, so concurrently start working on a poem about a creature who's not widely regarded as lovable, but whose life cycle and biology are nothing short of extraordinary. The European eel spawns in the Sargasso Sea, then travels several thousand kilometres to the coast of Europe in its larval stage, where it enters estuaries and begins to migrate upstream. Years later, as a sexually mature adult, it leaves its freshwater home again and begins the long journey back to its spawning grounds in the western Atlantic. As if this reproductive cycle weren't wondrous enough, I learn that in its young, elver stage when it starts its upstream migration, it's so transparent that a newspaper could conceivably be read through its body. I decide, therefore, to write an eel-shaped, fantastical poem about all that it might be possible to see through the body of an elver — not only information relating to its life history and migration, but, most critically, the various threats to its survival.

It strikes me, too, as I work through the first few drafts of 'Glass', that the poem has taken on the structure of a list, and that many of the other residency poems I've thus far written could also be described as variants on the list form. Since the project began with my being presented with a list of Thirty Threatened Species, this feels serendipitously appropriate. I wonder if it might be possible for me to experiment further with the list format, bending and stretching its boundaries, in some of the remaining poems.

As a means of feeling my way into the writing of poem number twenty-two, I'm all set to scribble another list, this time of the brainstorming kind. But having trawled around in my mind for some poetry-appropriate particulars about the Atlantic cod, hardly one of the most obscure of the thirty species, and landed only a few random early childhood memories, I'm thinking this list isn't likely to be a very substantial one.

I remember Friday school lunches — two cod fish fingers and a gloopy dollop of parsley sauce.

I remember overhearing the phrase 'Cod Wars' and picturing fish swimming into battle, weapons weirdly wedged between their fins.

I remember my mother always insisting on ordering posh scampi instead of cod at the chip shop since 'Cod's a common fish.'

I remember grimaceful facefuls of cod liver oil.

And then I summon up an adult memory too. Travelling through Newfoundland and listening, time and again, to conversations about the 'cod moratorium' — the fact that cod stocks on the Grand Banks had collapsed due to decades of over-exploitation, resulting in the Canadian Government issuing a cod fishing ban. Thousands of Newfoundlanders consequently lost their jobs, unemployment rocketed and many left the province to seek work on the Canadian mainland. As I travelled, I also became aware of former fishermen diversifying, particularly into the tourist industry — setting up B&Bs; foraging for partridgeberries, bakeapples and crowberries with which to make and sell jam; performing in dinner theatre shows; reinventing themselves as folk artists like Ben Ploughman, of sperm whale skeleton fame. Some had undoubtedly made a success of these alternative enterprises, but more than ten years on from the moratorium, there was still considerable lingering bitterness. Though I sympathised with the ex-fishermen with whom I came into contact, I also found myself grieving for the fish whose population had been so decimated — a population once so plentiful that in the fifteenth century, a basket lowered over the side of a boat into the sea would be drawn up overflowing with cod.

As far as the progress of the poem goes, in addition to offering snapshots of my limited connection with, and knowledge of, cod from different stages in my life in the first two stanzas, I feel I need to move on from these partial memories and attempt to properly engage with the fish in their natural environment too. Thus, in the final verse of 'Song', I shift into a more celebratory tone, and end by describing the cod performing their post-courtship spawning ritual.

'There.'
　'Where?'
　'To the left, past the buoy.'
　'Which buoy?'
　'The black one.'
Ten pairs of binoculars swing towards the stretch of sun-marbled sea beyond the squat, white lighthouse.
　'Again!'
　'Where?'
　'Bit further over.'
　'You sure?'
　'Dunno. Maybe.'
　'Missed it.'
Tuts and sighs.
　I rest my binoculars on my lap and scan, instead, with the naked eye, all the way from the foot of the cliffs on which we're perching to the smear of horizon. I linger on a circling gang of gannets, waiting to see if they're about to plunge-dive, as they're

often a good indicator that marine mammals are also feeding in the area. But the wind-riffled sea and angle of the sun are making it tricky to sight anything today. Each heave of wave could be a fin. Each cloud shadow the suggestion of a being beneath the surface.

I'm on day three of WOW Cetaceans — WOW being the felicitous acronym for Wildlife Observer Wales — an innovative course co-run by Pembrokeshire College and Sea Trust, a local marine wildlife charity. It's the first of a number of residency-relevant courses and workshops that I'll be attending over the next few months. Each morning, we've had lectures on such topics as cetacean biology and the conservation value of doing land-based observations and, today, an exam in which our ability to ID different species of dolphins, porpoises and whales from photos of their dorsal fins has been tested. Then, each afternoon, we've been transported to a different spot on the Pembrokeshire or Ceredigion coast in the hope of spying some of those dorsal fins for ourselves. Yesterday, we were in New Quay and, in contrast to my boat trip experience of the previous summer, a pod of twelve bottlenose dolphins appeared the instant we clambered out of the minibus. They put on a classic display of breaching, tail-slapping and leaping several metres clear of the water while we walked with gasps and oohs and aahs, as if echolocating our way from car park to harbour.

Yet this afternoon, the mood of my fellow students is more muted. We've travelled to Strumble Head, all wave-crash and crags and splintered-off islets, with the aim of seeing harbour porpoises feeding in the tidal races off the headland, but very few of my companions seem excited about it. I can't help but feel expectant, though, having enjoyed many stellar Strumble spectacles in the past, be it the squill-speckled cliffs of spring, the dusk processions of thousands of Manx shearwaters streaming home to their burrows on Skomer in summer, or grey seal pups emerging from their autumn birth-caves.

'There!'

'Where?'

'*There!* Where my finger is.'

'Dunno where you're pointing.'

Clipboards and binoculars to hand, we're all sitting in a row in front of the wartime lookout that's evolved into a peacetime wildlife-watching hide. As an additional part of our assessment for the course, we have to conduct a series of short surveys, filling in recording forms with sea state, wind force and visibility information, as well as any harbour porpoise sightings.

'You got a signal?'

'One bar. You?'

'Nah. Gutted.'

In addition to filling in the front of my recording forms, I've been scrawling ideas for my next poem on the back. Until today, I hadn't really grasped the fact that unofficial rankings seem to exist as far as sightings of cetaceans are concerned. I'm well familiar with people prizing the drama of dolphins of course, but didn't expect there to be such subdued enthusiasm for the harbour porpoise. Yes, it's smaller and less obviously active and showy but if most of the folk who've elected to take a marine wildlife course are a bit lukewarm about seeing it, how on earth might others, with no history of interest in oceanic life, be persuaded to care about its conservation and campaign against the pollution and gillnetting that trigger its decline?

I figure that my poem will need to offer an alternative scenario in the form of a marine mammal-monitoring novice whose initial disaffection gives way to joy when he records a harbour porpoise sighting for the first time. I'm thinking I'll write it in the form of a haibun, a combination of prose and haiku, so that at the very instant the creature's glimpsed, the boundary between prose and poetry can dissolve, the transition into poetry, coupled with the shift from the traditional haiku form, reflecting the volunteer sea-watcher's heightened delight.

'See that?'

'What?'

'There! Miles off.'

'Where d'you mean?'

'Like, halfway to the horizon.'

I'm also hoping that aspects of the environment, from the wind to the buoys to the clouds, will echo harbour porpoise biology in some way. Through these images, the reader will garner anatomical information — the fact that the porpoise has a rounded snout, rather than a pointed, dolphin-like beak, for example — as well as details about some of the perils it's facing. And in the process, I'd like to try to convey that all these landscape features are joining together in appreciation of the threatened cetacean.

'What d'you reckon?'

'Nah, that's not a porpoise, mate.'

'Can't see a thing.'

'How much longer?'

The harbour porpoise haibun, 'Volunteer', joins several other poems I've produced in the course of my MCS residency that are written from the perspective of a human or group of humans aspiring to watch, or already absorbed in watching, marine mammals or birds.

But what poem might result, I now start pondering, if I instead write from the point of view of a creature who's acutely aware that it's the object of human scrutiny?

What if I encourage the blue shark, a species that's been extensively tagged, tracked and studied, to express its thoughts on the experience of being so thoroughly monitored? Unlike some of the other shark species about whom I've written, much is known about the blue shark's life, its mating habits (such as the fact that females' skin is three times thicker than that of males because of the bites that the latter inflict) and migration patterns (mating in the northwest Atlantic and pupping in the northeast). I decide to imagine how the blue shark might feel about having the intimacies of its life exposed in this way. And what might its opinion be of humans who, on the one hand, carry out scientific studies to help with conservation, yet on the other, continue to kill up to twenty million of its kind each year?

I also decide there needs to be a progression in terms of my assigning a distinctive language to each creature in whose voice I'm choosing to write, mirroring their respective conservation statuses. Thus, the blue shark who's Near Threatened on the IUCN Red List will speak, in 'Watched', with a closer-to-human voice than the linguistically quirky porbeagle in 'Play', whose decline, and consequent Vulnerable conservation status, is more serious.

Before I reach poem number thirty, perhaps I'll write in the voice of another of the threatened creatures, perhaps one from the Critically Endangered section.

And perhaps there'll be nothing recognisably human about that creature's language at all.

I kneel on a patch of wet mud and tangled grass and move my nose towards the mossy rock in front of me. Balanced atop the rock is a tarry black dropping, no more than a few inches long.

I take a tentative sniff. Not an unpleasant smell. Not mink, then.

Another sniff. Quite aromatic, actually. Vaguely reminiscent of Earl Grey tea.

I raise my head a little, switch from ID-ing via nose to eyes. There are bones in there, definitely. And fish scales? Not sure. But taking into account the smell, as well as its prominent position on a rock for others to discover, I'm guessing this is the shit I've been hoping to find.

Otter.

I've learnt a lot about droppings in the five hours since this Otter Ecology training day with the Wildlife Trust of South and West Wales got underway. We spent all morning in the classroom, peering into petri dishes containing spraint in various stages of decomposition, as well as fused amphibian bones and other excreted prey remains. We studied a number of slides showing holts (dens that may be under the roots of trees such as oaks and sycamores) and hovers (temporary resting places like riverbank hollows) too. And now, for the afternoon session, we've left the classroom behind and travelled to the Neath Valley to hunt for field signs and try to apply all we've learnt.

I was initially surprised to find the Eurasian otter on the Thirty Threatened Species list, not because I thought its numbers are too abundant for it to be included — its near extinction in the UK by the late 1970s, in part due to the widespread use of river-polluting toxic pesticides, has been well documented — but because I think of it much more as a creature of rivers than sea.

'Oh, there are certainly coastal otters,' the course instructor, a retired university professor, tells me when I quiz him about this. 'They just need regular access to freshwater too, to desalt their fur.'

Here, in this inland Welsh valley, there's freshwater in abundance, with the presence of the placid Neath Canal as well as the more restive adjacent river, the Afon Nedd. Wellied and waterproof-jacketed, our instructor strides alongside first one, then the other, leading us down boggy banks and under stone bridges, beating paths through brambles, pointing out five-toed prints in the mud, as well as moss mounded by otters and crowned with spraint to act as a sign heap.

Though many members of the group are longing to spot an otter, and have travelled from as far away as Kent in the hope that the course will enable them to do so, I find, as the afternoon progresses, that unseeing is every bit as satisfying. Recognising field signs — not spying the actual creature, yet perceiving it on another level by becoming aware of its habits and movements — pleases me hugely. And I know this will form the focus of the otter poem, 'Watch', I'll be aiming to write.

My human ability to perceive, however, has frustrating limitations. 'There are over one hundred letters in the scent alphabet of otters!' our instructor declares, as I kneel to ID yet another spraint specimen, this one growing ash-grey with age. An otter would be able to read so much about its fellow creatures and the immediate environment — *I'm a dominant male* or *I'm a female in oestrus* or *There are no fish here* — simply by sniffing this shit, while I can't even detect traces of Earl Grey any more.

Long after the Otter Ecology day course is over, I ponder on how I can integrate this idea into my poem too, and eventually come up with a potential structure. It will be another in my wildlife-watching series, yes, but wildlife-watching with a twist: over the course of the poem, the human observer will shapeshift into otter, acquiring its keen sensory capacity and forging, in the process, an intimate bond between watcher and watched.

Having written this poem, I think back to my third collection of poetry, *skindancing*, which is entirely themed around human-animal metamorphosis, drawing on shapeshifting myths and fairytales from a range of different cultures, from Celtic to Inuit to Norse. Myth has featured prominently in my other collections too, yet so far, it hasn't had much of a presence in my Thirty Threatened Species poems. Why, I wonder, should this be? Because myth seems too rooted in human culture, and the threatened species have been so damaged by humans that they deserve to take centre stage and be seen in their own right rather than through an anthropocentric lens? Possibly. Yet I've long felt that engagement with myth in the context of poetry can facilitate relationship with the more-than-human too, helping to re-establish the connection with the wider natural world, where we're just one animal among many, that Western culture has lost.

I also feel there's something enduring and therefore reassuring about myth, attributes that are urgently needed in this era of mass extinction, galloping climate change, political and ecological collapse. Linking us with the past, myth offers a sense of stability too, a structure to cling to as we career headlong into our fractured future. In addition, myth originally functioned as a means of trying to explain the nature of the world and how it came into existence, and in these loss-infused times, we need new explanations, new stories, to help us fathom the crisis into which we've catapulted ourselves and our fellow beings.

The next poem I'll write, then, about the endangered loggerhead turtle, will revolve around a myth that has fascinated me for quite a while: the Native American creation story of the world turtle balancing the earth on its back. Into the framework of this myth, I'll aim to interweave some loggerhead turtle science, such as the fact that their bodies are important habitats for a wide range of other creatures, and references to the activities and coastal developments that are causing their demise. And ultimately, 'Create' will reference the salt secretions that are squeezed from their eyes, which we anthropomorphise as tears.

'So, finally, what's Spike's favourite activity?'

'He likes to run on the beach,' says the woman sitting closest to the workshop tutor, with not even a smidgen of uncertainty in her voice. 'He's got a blue ball and he likes to chase it on the sand.'

'Sausage,' declares one of the few men in the group. 'He says he likes to eat sausage.'

'He loves to snuggle on the sofa with his humans.'

I half-close my eyes again, breathe deep and focus on trying to tune into the bright-eyed, prick-eared terrier who's made himself at home in our workshop space, sniffing the shoes of each participant in turn and nosing in our rucksacks. A phrase scampered into my mind as soon as the tutor posed her final question but in spite of her urging us all to go with the first, and strongest, piece of information we receive because it's likely to be the most authentic, I really can't bring myself to speak it aloud. Everyone else is coming out with plausible doggy kinds of enjoyments while my contribution's going to sound completely ludicrous.

'I'm getting that he likes to run on the beach too. But it's not a blue ball he plays with, it's red.'

'I'm seeing a fire.' This comes from the woman to my right, fingering her rose quartz necklace. 'A big, roaring, open fire. Spike loves to sleep in front of it.'

All eyes turn to me.

Shall I mumble it? Babble it? Say it so quietly that no-one will be able to hear? Beg to be excused?

The workshop tutor's gaze flickers to my name badge and she gives an encouraging smile. 'Susan?'

'Um. Ducks,' I say. 'Spike — um — he likes to play with ducks.'

Like mostly everyone else in the room, I've enrolled for this weekend workshop in Animal Communication because I recently watched an online documentary about the pioneering work of Anna Breytenbach, the South African interspecies communicator and animal activist. Breytenbach uses her ability to psychically dialogue with non-human animals in educational, conservation and rehabilitation contexts and believes that we all have the capacity to connect with other creatures in this way. In the light of my vacillation over poetry's suitability for inspiring action for change, I'm keen to discover more about another process that works, like poetry, on the intuitive, visceral level, in the hope of gaining new insights and recovering some of my old conviction.

Having spent the first morning of the workshop learning some basic telepathic communication techniques, we've since been absorbed in trying to put what we've learnt into practice. Several dogs, known as our 'guest teachers', including Spike the terrier, have been invited along, and we've even been encouraged to attempt to communicate with a pet python whose serene energy while she rested on the tutor's lap coaxed both a snake-phobic workshopper out of the corner and unbidden tears from my eyes. I've been shifting between conflicting emotional states all weekend, in fact, feeling alternately uncomfortable, elated, intensely sceptical and a hard-core telepathy devotee. I've veered between failing to receive any communication at all, feeling sure that I must be inventing everything, and gleaning occasional bits of information that the tutor insists are spot-on but I fear may just be lucky guesses.

It's clear that I'll be processing my experiences from the weekend for quite some time. And even before the workshop's over and even though I haven't had the chance to try to communicate with a marine creature yet, I'm already processing ideas for my next poem. With modern-day interspecies communicators in mind, as well as mythological figures such as Orpheus, I've decided I'm going to write, in 'Charmed', about a woman who has a knack for attracting animals of all kinds to her side. Her gift extends to calling the ninth-largest creature on the planet, the swift-swimming sei whale, hunted almost to extinction in the nineteenth and twentieth centuries, from thousands of miles away across the ocean. This woman now craves to gain the trust of, and forge a genuine connection with, the sei whale and, in the first instance, aims to impart that not all members of the human race tend towards violence. Her hope is that an increasing number of people will seek simply to see, wonder at, and initiate peaceful communication with, their fellow creatures as a first step towards protecting them.

'So, we've heard about all sorts of activities that Spike might like doing,' the workshop tutor continues, once everyone in the group has spoken, 'from chasing balls to playing with ducks.'

Quick ripple of giggles, including an embarrassed one from me.

'So why don't we get verification from Spike's guardian. Ron?'

We all shift our attention to the baseball-capped man who's been sitting in silence at the front of the room. He stops fiddling with the clasp of the dog lead on his lap and sits up straighter. 'Well, he likes doing a lot of the things you've talked about, to be honest. Sausage — he loves a bit of sausage.'

Smug smile from the guy who mentioned it and an ultra-pronounced ear prick from Spike who, having heard the word, is now on high sausage alert.

'He loves chasing balls too, don't you, Spikey? In the park, though, not on the beach.'

The woman next to the tutor shakes her head and frowns. 'I'm sure Spike said he likes running on the beach. I got the clearest message.'

'But what he likes best of all is his walks up at the lake.' Ron's eyes rove round the room and come to rest on me. 'All he wants to do is play. The ducks. We just can't stop him.'

'Good morning, Mister Magpie — how's your wife and family?'

Most mornings before breakfast, my mother, still dressing-gowned and hair-netted, would raise the kitchen blinds and scan the whole of the back garden, from bird table to ash tree, privet to patio, bird bath to silver birch, in the hope of catching sight of a pair of magpies for good luck. If she saw only 'one for sorrow' rather than 'two for joy', her scanning of the garden would take on a more urgent air, her gaze darting towards every leaf flicker and hedge twitch, expelling an exclamation of despair when she spied but a blackbird or crow. If, after several more minutes of trying, she had to concede that only one magpie was indeed present, she'd go through the ritual of greeting him, enquiring after the health of his spouse and offspring, then saluting him, fingers to brow, all in an attempt to fend off the bad luck that the sighting of a single magpie was supposed to bring.

I'm reminded of my mother's superstitious brand of bird-watching when attending another animal communication workshop, this time in rural Hampshire. Rather than focusing on further telepathic techniques, this one has a more shamanic emphasis. Since I've previously been a member of a shamanic journeying circle over a period of several years, the part where we're encouraged to meet and engage with our Power Animals feels very familiar. Learning to recognise, and attempting to interpret, messages from any wild animals, including bees, butterflies and birds, that we may encounter in our daily lives, however, is new territory for me.

We're ushered outdoors for much of the afternoon session and urged to keep all our senses open to potential communications coming from objects associated with animals, such as moulted feathers, as well as from animals themselves. But with The British Open Polo Championship taking place barely a jackdaw's wingbeat away from where we're wandering, the only messages I get are of the ostentatious human kind.

Post-workshop, though, I do some wider reading into the subject of animal signs and augury from classical antiquity onwards. In ancient Rome, it seems that significant decisions were often made based on interpretations of the appearance and movement of animals, especially birds. All manner of information would be taken into account, including the sector of sky where the birds were spotted, and the direction in which, and from which, they were flying. The number of birds that appeared was also of consequence and this prompts me to think about writing an augury-themed poem about the velvet scoter, an endangered sea duck on my Marine Conservation Society list. What, I want to consider, might rapidly declining numbers of velvet scoters indicate or foretell?

I return to my mother's 'one for sorrow, two for joy' rhyme for the structure of 'Augur', though opt for a reverse version where the numbers of velvet scoters decrease, rather, than increase, as a result of the marine pollution, loss of breeding and wintering habitats, and other pressures from which the duck is suffering.

Still two poems to go.

Still a little early, then, to do a grand overview of my MCS residency and the journey on which it's taken me. Yet as I wander round the seminar room and convince sundry Professors, several vets and miscellaneous postgrads to close their eyes and bury their faces in the clumps of seaweed that I gathered from the tideline of the Solway Firth on my way up to Glasgow yesterday, I can't help but reflect that it's brought me to places I could never have imagined.

'Remember to keep your eyes tightly shut for the first part of this exercise. I want you to disconnect from the visual and explore the object that I've placed in your hands solely through the sense of smell.'

I've recently revelled in the experience of being a student on a string of residency-related courses, but today, I've returned to facilitating a marine-themed workshop of my own. And having dabbled for a while in myth and the mystical, I'm back in a more rigorous academic environment — though with every desk in the room freckled with sand, and wafts of holiday sea-saltiness in the air, rigour's not entirely evident right now.

'Keep working with your object, please. Even if you think you've discovered multiple layers of smells, try to extract something more.'

On the back of my contribution to 'Cold Blood(ed)' at Cardiff University six or so months ago, I was asked by Erica Fudge, director of the British Animal Studies Network, to offer a writing workshop at the organisation's next conference, 'Smelling', here at the University of Strathclyde. And I'm feeling both honoured and on edge to have also been invited to deliver one of the conference's plenary sessions. Taking the form of a poetry performance, my presentation will include the sharing of a new poem, commissioned by the Network and responding to the smelling theme.

Having managed to persuade all my workshop participants to produce their own smelling-as-a-marine-creature poem, I try to focus on the afternoon's papers and discussions but though each promises to be fascinating, my pre-performance nerves somewhat blur the contents. An anatomy of olfaction. Dogs reading their pee-mails. Bloodhounds tracking Jack the Ripper. Beekeepers having the ability to smell 'happy queens'. Freebie sachets of pheromones to calm our companion animals, which I wish could be used on me.

My session's scheduled for the early evening, immediately

preceding the conference buffet, and as I step onto the stage, I'm wondering if my new poem's anywhere near compelling enough to hold the attention of a lecture hall full of hungry, and probably pretty weary, delegates. The final shark on the Thirty Threatened Species list, the slender, long-lived tope, has been lurking and circling in the waters of my writing mind for some time now. Finding a fresh angle from which to write about each of the sharks on the list has been one of my biggest residency challenges, especially as they all face similar perils — from gillnet and longline fishing to overhunting for their fins and liver oil. The smelling theme of this conference, though, has provided me with a refreshingly different route into shark poem number nine.

'As I'm sure you all know, sharks are renowned for having an unparalleled sense of smell,' I begin, 'so I've decided to imagine a whole range of things, both real and surreal, that the tope shark might be able to scent. The majority of them relate to indications that the ocean and its creatures, including the tope herself, are steadily being wrecked by human activities and behaviour.'

Swift scan of the raked rows of seating. Good. No-one's sneaking out for a mini-samosa just yet.

'Because 'Stench' is originating as a performance piece, to be listened to here at the conference, I've aimed to create a chain of near rhymes, assonance and words packed with plosives so that you're all drawn through the poem from sound echo to sound echo, just as the tope shark is drawn, by her extraordinary olfactory ability, through the water from smell to smell.'

Intro done. Here goes.

I swim further upriver into sound when I come to work on my final poem, about the critically endangered sturgeon. The ongoing survival of this majestic, prehistoric fish couldn't be more precarious. Fossilised sturgeon remains have been discovered in deposits from over fifty million years ago and it was widespread throughout Europe for centuries, including in UK rivers such as the Severn, Avon and Thames. Yet now, only one declining breeding population can be found across the entire continent, in the Garonne River in France. Ironically, it's popularly known as the common sturgeon: like the skate and the seal, two other creatures on the Thirty Threatened Species list to whose names we've affixed the adjective 'common', the sturgeon is now anything but.

Remembering that five or six poems ago, I speculated that

I might at some point experiment with writing in a critically endangered creature's voice, I begin to craft an elegy in a language that bears no resemblance whatsoever to human communication. I end up inventing three sturgeon dialects, in fact, with a different sonic landscape coming to the fore in each to reflect the various environments that the sturgeon inhabits and the migratory pattern that it follows over the course of its lifetime. However, human intervention exists even at the linguistic level, as I also provide a translation, umpteen footnotes and an overblown analysis of the sturgeon's language, all of which add up to being far longer than the original poem.

I write it slowly, interrogating myself over the choice of every phrase, compulsively tweaking, loath to finish and let it go. 'Plibble', poem number thirty, represents my last chance to highlight the plight of the Threatened Species and having reached it, I don't feel relieved or satisfied — just hyper-concerned.

Have I done each species justice? Said all I hoped to say? Focused too much on loss? Explored too few solutions?

And now the composing of the poems is over, what next?

Zipped to the chin and woolly-hatted, I'm trudging through mud, leaning into the fading light and strong southwesterly. From time to time, I stop, wipe my wind-weepy eyes with gloved fingers and look out at the boisterous sea. Apart from a few squalling herring gulls, there's no sign of any of the wildlife I relish seeing in other seasons of the year. No nesting fulmars bill-fencing. No compass jellyfish navigating turquoise summer waves. No migrant wheatears foraging for beetles on the cliff top. No curious seal pups nosing floating hunks of driftwood following an autumn storm.

Drafts of many of the Thirty Threatened Species poems formed in my head as I walked this length of coast between Ceibwr Bay and the collapsed cave-cum-blowhole known as the Witch's Cauldron several times a week during the course of my MCS residency. And today, a few months on, it's thoughts about ordering the poems in preparation for publication that are accompanying my walk. In addition to grouping them according to the IUCN Red List categories, from Least Concern to Critically Endangered, I'm hoping that other narratives will emerge as the manuscript takes shape — the movement, for example, from the portrayal of more familiar creatures and the inescapable presence of humans in the early poems to the focus on scarcely known and less accessible species in those poems that feature later in the text. There's the placement of Pat's images, and the additional storyline that they provide, to consider too — broadly, a journey from presence to absence. In her final image, the angel shark doesn't appear at all. Instead, we see just the ripples of water that remain after the creature has passed — or perhaps, in view of its extinct-in-the-North-Sea status, passed away.

I edge carefully along the short stretch of diverted coast path — created just a couple of weeks ago when a section of cliff, weakened by rainwater run-off from the adjacent fields, crumbled into the sea — and then swing towards the narrow valley of Cwm Pen-wern, near the mouth of which the crater of the Witch's Cauldron is seething with the rising tide. The wind's gusting so fiercely here that spume's being tugged up from the sea and flung into the air to accumulate on the cliff top. For a moment, I have the sensation that I'm walking through a snowstorm — which seems to be the closest that this warming, wet, west coast ever gets to snow now in winter.

Squatting next to a gorse bush to minimise wind-buffeting, I peek over the rim of the Cauldron and watch the waves rampaging and rearranging the rocks of its floor a few hundred feet below. Although it sounds a bit drama queenly, I feel like I've been perched on the edge of a precipice quite a few times since I embarked on my residency. Not just in terms of the challenges of the writing but also on account of the conferences at which I've stretched myself to perform, the sometimes out-of-my-comfort-zone courses I've opted to take, and the constant striving to concoct new ways for workshoppers to connect with cold-blooded creatures. Because of the emotional challenge of engaging with the loss theme too. And, most fundamental of all, because of working to prove to scientists, academics, marketing folk, and audience members at every event in which I've been involved, the value of poetry in helping to raise awareness of vulnerable marine wildlife.

With dusk having taken over from day, I really should think about making my way back to Ceibwr, but my mind's now snagged on the activist poetry theme like the sleeve of a fleece on a branch of gorse and I'm disinclined to move. My faith in poetry's ability to effect meaningful change went through a shaky phase midway through the residency when I became overwhelmed by the global scale of the marine debris problem but gradually, thanks to conversations with colleagues, nights of insomniac pondering, an initiation into the world of animal communication and a re-acquaintance with the transformative power of myth, I've reached a more positive plateau again. Poetry on its own can't, of course, spark a revolution in government policy or the plastics and fishing industries but I've seen it inspire many critical shifts in awareness and attitude on an individual level, and the cumulative effect of these, alongside other small-scale movements for change, can have major significance. Which is why, once the Thirty Threatened Species book is published, I'll be immersing myself in the next phase of the project, performing and sharing the poetry far and wide, equipped with the conviction that one of the best ways of defending marine — or, indeed, any — species, is by reconnecting our imaginations to them.

Over to the west, near the winking lighthouse of Strumble Head, a thin stripe of day is still lighting the sky. I stand up, stretch stiff legs and regretfully turn my back on it as I start walking.

And the sea — beneath the surface of which I can now picture harbour porpoises feeding, pink sea fans branching and occasional porbeagles teasing strands of kelp — shrugs off the deepening dark and follows me home.